Speaking And Listening

By Murray Suid
Illustrated by Corbin Hillam

Publisher: Roberta Suid
Editor: Bonnie Bernstein
Designer: David Hale

ISBN 0-912107-03-0

Printed in the United States of America

9 8 7 6 5 4 3 2 1

CONTENTS

Worksheets 47

55 worksheets to accompany lessons

Bulletin Boards 103

INTRODUCTION

Showing, telling, and listening are skills students can learn. Virtually all students can be taught:
- how to give clear and entertaining speeches;
- how to have fun giving—and listening to —speeches;
- how to use speaking and listening as tools for learning, working, and serving the community.

When I say that virtually all students can develop these skills, "virtually all" includes the shyest and most stage-frightened kids you have.

This assertion comes from personal experience. Some years ago I was hired to speak at a series of educational workshops around the country. Five minutes into my first presentation, I fainted. I don't meant that I got a little nervous or confused or flustered.

I fainted!

You may not believe it, but there were plenty of eyewitnesses. Too many, in fact, for my taste.

But the story does not end with my lying on the stage like a sack of mashed potatoes. With the help of my employer (who was there), and my teaching colleagues (who were there), I eventually learned how to get my fear of facing an audience under control.

Since the day of that rather unpleasant fainting experience, I have given over a thousand presentations. Dale Carnegie I'm not nor will I ever be. But I can get up in front of a crowd and tell people what I'm thinking. Usually I come away feeling good about myself and feeling that the audience learned something useful, or at least had a good time.

The "secret" to my modest success is diabolically simple and very ancient: Practice.

The form of the practice presentations doesn't matter. Whatever I'm doing up there—reading a speech, talking off the cuff, answering questions, narrating a set of slides, taking part in a panel—it all adds up to greater and greater confidence.

So, this is a book of varied, and often fun, practices that get kids to practice presenting themselves visually and aurally in lots of ways. It's organized alphabetically because there really is no one right place to start. Each activity, whether imitating animal voices or giving a formal speech, exercises most of the basic skills needed to make a competent, interesting presentation.

The book itself is divided into three sections. For starters, you'll find **lessons**, which describes activities, games, and general teaching strategies.

The next section is a collection of duplicatable **worksheets** students can use for independent study and practice.

The **bulletin board** section will help you create a motivational climate for experimenting with speaking and listening. Taping student performances can offer additional motivation, as well as feedback. If possible, provide each student with his or her individual tape. It can be used throughout the year and saved as an electronic souvenir of times spent in your class.

P.S. While working on this project, I came across a book that suggested an easy way to encourage reluctant speakers. Begin by asking them to state the thing they're most afraid of when contemplating giving a speech. When someone says, "I'm afraid I might faint in front of everybody," the teacher is supposed to say, "That's a silly fear. Have you ever heard of anyone actually fainting while giving a speech?"

The technique is supposed to work.

LESSONS

Airport Announcement Game

- following spoken directions
- making announcements

This activity is based on a real event witnessed by the author. It deepened his conviction that getting along in the modern world requires highly developed listening skills.

The scene was a departure lounge at a certain major airport. Passengers were waiting to board three flights through three side-by-side gates. The planes were scheduled to depart at exactly the same time.

When the moment for boarding came, the gate attendant for each flight began to call out instructions. Passengers had to sort out information concerning flight number, gate number, row number, class, special status (children traveling alone or others requiring assistance in boarding), and which door of the plane—front or rear—to board through. To call the resulting exodus a "stampede" would be to understate the chaos.

PLAYING THE AIRPLANE ANNOUNCEMENT GAME. Before the game starts, cut up copies of *Worksheet 1*, Airplane Boarding Passes. For young children, adapt the activity by simplifying the tickets and directions.

Choose three students to act as *boarding gate announcers* and three more as *boarding pass checkers*. Each announcer-checker team should stand by a "gate" labeled with one of three flight numbers. (The gate can be a stool or a desk.) Give a boarding pass to each student acting as a "passenger."

When the game begins, all students holding boarding passes should be seated. The three gate announcers will read from *Worksheet 2*, Airplane Boarding Announcement Script.

When "passengers" hear their flight and row number called for boarding, they will walk up to the correct gate and hand their tickets to the ticket checker. (For a less active version, students can simply hold up their tickets at the right moment. The ticket checkers can do the moving.)

CREATING OTHER BOARDING SCRIPTS. Students can use *Worksheets 1* and *2* as models to create tickets and announcement scripts for other transportation.

NAME
Boarding Passes

flight #235 London Row 1 C	flight #238 Rome Row 1 C	flight #128 Mexico City Row 1 F
flight #235 London Row 2 B	flight #238 Rome Row 2 D	flight #128 Mexico City Row 2 A
flight #235 London Row 4 G	flight #238 Rome Row 3 E X	flight #128 Mexico City Row 3 G
flight #235 London Row 10 D X	flight #238 Rome Row 12 F	flight #128 Mexico City Row 11 B
flight #235 London Row 12 A	flight #238 Athens Row 14 G	flight #128 Mexico City Row 14 G X
flight #235 London Row 17 J	flight #238 Athens Row 15 A X	flight #128 Mexico City Row 17 J
flight #235 London Row 20 H	flight #238 Athens Row 17 B	flight #128 Mexico City Row 19 E
flight #235 London Row 21 H X	flight #238 Athens Row 19 H	flight #128 Mexico City Row 21 F
flight #235 London Row 22 B	flight #238 Athens Row 20 C X	flight #128 Lima Row 22 D X
flight #235 London Row 24 F X	flight #238 Athens Row 24 A	flight #128 Lima Row 24 A X

Animal Voices

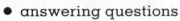

- listening
- using the voice
- giving oral reports

In the following activity, it's not just "Monkey see, monkey do." It's also "Monkey hear, monkey talk." The idea is for students to give authentic imitations of animal voices.

Most kids learn animal talk—*moo*, *arf*, and so on—from other human beings. But to really speak like the creatures, one really needs to hear the words directly from, pardon the expression, the horse's mouth. This is not only more fun; it requires a much higher level of listening.

IMITATING ANIMALS. Even if you have a zoo nearby, there's no guarantee that the animals will oblige you with talk. For more efficiency, play a sound effects record or tape that features animal sounds. These are available in many large record stores. Especially dramatic are recordings of bird songs and whale talk. Whatever recording you get hold of, simply play it and then have the students, ensemble or solo, try to imitate the sounds.

GIVING ANIMAL REPORTS WITH SOUNDS. Have each student specialize in imitating a particular animal. The imitation animal talk can then be incorporated in an oral report about that creature.

Ask-Me-About-It Game

- answering questions
- conversing
- thinking on one's feet

Only one thing is worse than being asked a question whose answer you don't know: *not* being asked a question about a subject you're an expert on. While there's no easy way out for the first problem, the Ask-Me-About-It Game does solve the second. Ask me how to play it and I'll tell you.

"How do you play Ask-Me-About-It?"

I'm glad you asked. It's easy. First, students pick topics they know a lot about. A topic can be something learned at school, such as the capitals of all the North American countries, or information about a personal experience; for example, a meeting with the mayor.

Next, each student makes a button that invites passers-by to ask about the subject. The buttons can be worn just around the classroom, throughout the school, at home, or in the community. The only requirement is that when someone asks, the student must answer the question.

Students might report on the kinds of questions they receive and how they answered them. You might even graph the number of questions inspired by each button.

Canned Orations

- reading speeches
- listening to master speakers
- letter writing

Some of the world's greatest literature is in the form of speeches. Few experiences will do more to ignite interest in public speaking than in hearing historic orations via recordings or reenactments.

PRESENTING GREAT PEOPLE GIVING GREAT SPEECHES. A number of important, contemporary speeches dealing with politics, science, current events, and the arts are available on records and tapes. With a little scrounging, you should be able to bring the likes of Neil Armstrong, President Kennedy, and Madame Curie into your classroom.

REENACTING SPEECHES. Reenact classic speeches such as "The Gettysburg Address" and "George Washington's Farewell Address." Even if students won't understand every word, they will be moved by it. However, since almost all of this material would be difficult for elementary students to read, invite guest performers, such as other teachers, high school drama students, and actors from local theaters.

FINDING MATERIAL. Unfortunately, you'll have a hard time finding anthologies of speeches suitable for an elementary grade audience. One source is contemporary politicians such as the mayor, Congressional representatives, and so on. You or your students could write to these individuals asking for texts of speeches that would be of interest to young people—for example, the dedication of a new bike lane system, a piece of legislation affecting pets, the welcoming to town of a celebrity.

Charades

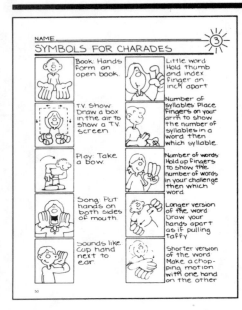

- using gestures
- listening
- breaking words into syllables

Parlors are obsolete and so are many of the games played in them. Fortunately, one such entertainment that's still around is *charades*. While this activity encourages even the shyest person to ham it up, there's more here than just fun and games. Many language skills get a workout: the leader must listen carefully to guesses from teammates; the teammates must speak clearly and listen to each other; and everyone learns about syllabification. (Try acting out *syllabification* without breaking the word into syllables.)

INTRODUCING THE GAME. The best way to teach charades to beginners is to stage a demonstration featuring experienced players. These can be kids who already know how to play, teachers, or aides. As for rules, there are but two:

1. The pantomimist must not speak or mouth any word.
2. The pantomimist must not use gestures to spell out letters.

There is, of course, a set of conventional signs for such stock phrases as "This is a book" or "I'm now going to act out the third word." *Worksheet 3*, Symbols for Charades, offers a visual glossary of these classic signs.

Finding items to act out is half the fun of the game. It also can introduce students to quotation books and other reference materials. So, if possible, have students do the work. Categories for collecting items include: titles of books, movies, TV shows, and songs (country and western music provides some dillies); quotations —serious and silly; slogans from the world of advertising and politics; and even phrases relating to school subjects, for example, "Reduce all fractions to their lowest common denominator" or "When two vowels go walking, the first one does the talking."

Cheers

- voice projection
- oral reading

When it comes to intensity and team work, no other speech format can match the cheer. (This is not a rainy-day project unless your gymnasium has lots of soundproofing.)

INTRODUCING CHEERING. If you were a cheerleader back in high school or college, you can teach the basics. If you don't know a pom-pon from a pomegranate, then you might consider inviting in a few cheerleaders from your local high school.

FINDING SOMETHING TO CHEER ABOUT. Cheers can be used to motivate everything from physical education to long division. The trouble is that the literature of cheering isn't vast, especially at the elementary level. If you really want students to cheer themselves into a frenzy about homework or improving their handwriting, you'll probably have to write your own cheers or, better, get your students to do it. For inspiration, feel free to use the original and uncopyrighted models below. They're sort of dumb, but then "Push 'em back, push 'em back, way back!" isn't Shakespeare either.

Two bits, four bits,
Six bits, a dollar.
If you can spell
Stand up and holler!

Hip, hip, hooray!
It's art today.
Drawing and sketching,
They're okay!

Come on everyone,
Time to be glad,
Open those math books
And add, add, add.

Homework, homework,
Make it rough.
_____ doesn't scare us,
'Cause our brains are tough.

Choral Reading

- listening
- overcoming stage fright
- oral reading

Choral reading offers the best proof that two (or more) heads can be better than one. Being surrounded by other speakers gives novices a sense of security and power that is a long time coming for the solo speaker. Live or taped choral performances, even those delivered by beginning readers, can be stunning.

GROUP SIZE. How big should a chorus be? There is no set size. To introduce the activity, you might work with the whole class. Later, groups with as few as two or three members can perform readings.

LEADERSHIP. Whatever the size of the chorus, having a leader is crucial. The leader's most important task —during rehearsals as well as performances—is to make sure the chorus begins together and proceeds at the correct pace. The leader also controls the volume which, like the pace, may change along the way. However, arm waving isn't needed. A subtle nod to begin is often all it takes. After modeling the leader's role, the teacher may encourage students to take over.

MATERIALS. While books of "special" choral materials exist, they aren't necessary. In fact, just about any text that reads well as a solo performance will do fine in the mouths of a group. Possible items that students as well as the teacher might collect are: poems, short stories, advertisements, newspaper articles, minutes of meetings, announcements, jokes, and even passages from a textbook.

DIVIDED READINGS. Most choruses speak in unison. However, "divided" or "sequenced" readings can be effective. For example, suppose your chorus intends to perform a limerick. You divide the group into halves (by sex or pitch). One half reads the first two lines of the poem; the other half the next two. The whole group reads line five. (Naturally, the script will have to indicate who reads what.) Not only will the audience be treated to vocal variety, but also a sense of "movement" —first voices on the left, then voices on the right, and then voices from both sides.

An extreme form of sequenced choral reading is to have each sentence of a story read by a single person. This would be a dramatic way to present stories written by your students.

Dial-a-Story

- oral reading
- storytelling

There's dial-a-this and dial-a-that. Why not a student-run, community-wide dial-a-story service that children —and adults—can call day or night?

Two San Jose, California, educators, Susan Bergtholdt and Mike Demko, created such a program featuring stories and poems read—and sometimes written—by students. The system, which also played readings by local celebrities, averaged 250 calls *a day*!

This activity requires a telephone answering machine. If your school has one that you can use at night or on weekends, you're in business. If it doesn't, maybe your PTA will buy you one. Models can be purchased for under $200 new and under $100 used. You might even be able to talk a local electronics store into contributing one. The publicity would pay off.

If your school is swimming in money, you can spend $1500 to get a heavy-duty, multi-line system (called a Theater Announcer). It's needed to handle the kind of volume the San Jose people achieved. (Susan Bergtholdt raised the money by having her district's eleven schools chip in about $100 a piece.)

Some of these machines limit the prerecorded message to thirty seconds. No problem. Simply offer very short works, such as jokes, brief parables, haiku, or "Ripley's Believe-It-Or-Not" type items. Even if your machine allows longer messages, it's a good idea to limit the time to three minutes or less. This way callers won't be frustrated by busy signals. Besides, all things equal, the shorter the story the higher the reading quality. And quality oral reading is what you're after.

PUBLICIZING THE SERVICE. Dial-a-Story programs grow mainly by word-of-mouth advertising. To start people talking, your students can create posters for display in other classrooms and in public places such as supermarkets and banks. Ads can also be written for the home-school newsletters in town. The publicity should tell potential callers the day or days when new programs are offered.

Dialogues

- overcoming stage fright
- developing a sense of timing
- giving oral reports

If it worked for Plato, Abbott and Costello, and Mr. Wizard, creating dialogues can work for your students, too.

COMEDY DIALOGUES. Much humorous literature is written for two performers. Knock-knock jokes fit into this category. So do innumerable silly riddles:

> Comedian 1: Why did the chicken cross the road?
> Comedian 2: Because she wore red suspenders.

To make sure neither comedian seems like a stupid stooge, the punch lines should be traded back and forth.

Comic strips such as *Peanuts* are an under-used source of amazingly literate dialogues. Kids can easily turn a three-panel strip into a vaudeville-type skit. Here's an example adapted from Johnny Hart's *B.C.*

> B.C.: (*carrying a pick and holding up a rock*) Glass! We've discovered *glass*.
> Peter: (looking disgustedly at the rock) Why you nincompoop! This is an ordinary diamond.

Don't-Look-at-Me Speeches

- overcoming stage fright
- concentrating on the voice
- listening

Being stared at is one of the major causes of stage fright. Here is a powerful solution: *no eye contact*.

The listeners close their eyes and put their heads down. The speaker then follows the standard speech procedures—enters, gets set, delivers the material, handles questions (if any), and exits. Throughout the presentation *no one looks at the speaker*.

Most material will work fine for the Don't-Look-at-Me Speech: jokes, personal narratives, songs, poems, and the like. While visual props are a no-no, the speaker can use sounds such as clapping or playing a musical instrument.

Earwitness

- listening
- reporting

To help students appreciate the richness of the aural environment, let them take part in an ear-oriented scavenger hunt. They can use *Worksheet 4*, Here's What I Heard, to keep track of experiences that ordinarily would have gone in one ear and out the other without ever being noticed. Share the results at show-and-tell time.

Eyewitness News Report

- extemporaneous speaking
- voicing the emotions
- reporting on current events

Usually a reporter is fortunate to be at the scene of a major calamity or other event. The following activities, however, remove the luck factor but, one hopes, not the thrills and chills.

INTRODUCING EYEWITNESS REPORTING. If possible, play recordings of authentic eyewitness news reports. Discuss the use of detail and voiced emotions. One place to get tapes is from a local news-oriented radio station; call up their public relations department.

PRACTICING EYEWITNESS REPORTING. Once students have a sense of what eyewitness reporting is all about, let them practice using one of the pictures on *Worksheet 5*, News Scenes, or *Worksheet 6*, Incredible News Scenes. Give each "reporter" exactly 60 seconds to translate the visual into action-packed words. If you don't want one student's performance to influence another's, simply have each child record the report in private. This has the extra advantage of making self-evaluation possible.

REPORTING ON LIVE EVENTS. Does your room face a street or other area where "things" will happen? If so, let students know that without warning you will thrust a microphone into someone's hands. At that point, the "reporter" must rush to the window and give a spontaneous, half-minute account of whatever is going on outside. Designs for the necessary props will be found on *Worksheet 19*, Making Microphones.

Guided Art

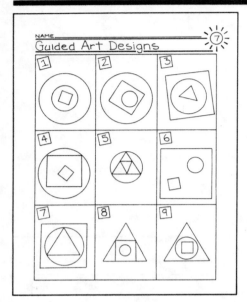

- giving directions
- following directions

The trouble with guiding someone else's fantasy is that the guide can't see the fantasy. This activity solves the problem. The basic idea is that the speaker studies a ready-made diagram and gives art instructions to the listener who draws the unseen picture. For art material, use the diagrams on *Worksheet 7*, Guided Art Designs, or have each speaker create his or her own pattern.

This project can be done while students sit at their desks, but for more drama, have several teams working simultaneously at the board. If you want to make the activity competitive, let each team work on the same diagram. If you want to remove competition, use different diagrams for each speaker-listener pair.

EASY VERSION. The listener-drawer can see his or her work as it's being drawn. This way, if the leader says, "Draw a square," the drawer can watch himself or herself do the work.

MORE CHALLENGING (AND MORE ENTERTAINING) VERSION. Don't attempt this variation until students have plenty of experience with the easy version. Assuming the students are ready, here's how to play:

The person doing the drawing wears a paper bag and therefore receives no visual feedback on the execution of directions. It is up to the speaker to give much more detailed guiding:

> "Now you'll draw a square inside the circle. Are you ready? Okay, now move your chalk to your left. Down a little. Up a little. Fine. Now slowly make a circle. Hold it! You're curving in—I mean down —too much. Move it more to the left. That's right..."

Naturally, the finished drawing will be rougher when rendered blindfolded but the speaker-listener pair will learn a lot more about the nature of spoken communication.

Hands Up Listening Game

- asking questions
- listening

Here's a game that not only exercises questioning and listening skills, but also shows the players their commonalities and uniquenesses.

PLAYING THE BASIC VERSION. Before the game starts, the leader prepares a series of "personal experience" questions for the audience. Depending on grade level, the list may contain 5, 10, or 15 questions. During the game, the leader rattles off these questions. Whoever can answer in the affirmative raises a hand.

> Who's left-handed? (Lefties' hands go up.)
>
> Who has a first name? (Everybody should raise a hand.)
>
> Whose first, middle, and last names taken together contain all the vowels? (Maybe no hands are raised.)
>
> Who has seen both the Atlantic and the Pacific oceans?
>
> Who owns three pets?
>
> Who has never tasted snails?
>
> Who has received a letter from a foreign country?

This sounds simple, and it is. The fun comes from seeing how quickly the questions can be fired off. After a little bit of practice, the game should be played at a breakneck pace with hands darting up and down as if they belonged to bidders at an auction.

ADDING WRINKLES. The leader is challenged to come up with questions that will a) get everybody's hand up; or b) keep everybody's hand down; c) get only boys' or only girls' hands up; or d) get any other prespecified group of hands up.

How-To-Do-It Speeches

- sequencing ideas
- speaking from notes
- teaching

Quite a few writers have looked for easy laughs by publishing children's confused efforts to explain such skills as making scrambled eggs or taking a bath. These supposedly funny books almost make it seem that kids are muddle-headed by nature. Of course, they're not. Given some guided practice, even very young children can learn to give clear, well-organized instructions.

DEMONSTRATING GIVING INSTRUCTIONS. If you want students to get good at giving instructions, provide them with plenty of models. Demonstrations should cover everything from cooking to making paper airplanes to throwing a football. Besides yourself, use a variety of demonstrators, such as other teachers, community experts, and older students.

LEARNING FROM A READY-MADE SCRIPT. A structured way to teach direction-giving skills is to have students work with a ready-made script. *Worksheet 8*, How to Make a Peanut Butter Sandwich, gives students practice in identifying key steps in an activity, arranging these steps in a logical order, and narrating the sequence.

The directions on the sheet call for cutting apart the pictures and reassembling them. With young children, the teacher may wish to handle the cutting task. In this case, simply give each child an envelope with the "steps" inside.

The worksheet encourages students to draw their own step-by-step instructional scripts. These can be presented by the writer or exchanged with a partner who will teach from the script. This second option should motivate students to be even more careful with the way they draw and caption their scripts.

CREATING A HOW-TO-DO-IT LESSON. As with all other forms of "theater," teaching requires planning and practice. *Worksheet 9*, How to Teach People to Do Anything, covers the basic steps for creating and testing an instructional routine. To help students get the most from this recipe, model its use by teaching a real skill, such as using the overhead projector.

GIVING HOW-NOT-TO-DO-IT DIRECTIONS. As a fun spinoff, students can write and deliver how-*not*-to-do-it instructions.

Introductory Speeches

- researching
- scripting

By teaching students how to give introductory speeches, you can vastly increase the opportunities for speech practice in your room.

INTRODUCING INTRODUCING. While introductions are almost always short, they do require careful preparation. *Worksheet 10*, How to Put the Spotlight on Someone Else, is a reusable fill-in recipe that covers the two basic steps. To have fun while practicing the format, students can introduce speeches that *might have been* delivered by a fantasy character such as Scrooge or by an historic figure such as Susan B. Anthony.

INTRODUCING REAL SPEAKERS. Once students have written and delivered imaginary introductions, let them put their skills to work. Three categories of real speakers who might need introducing are:

1) *Other students*. If Jane is giving an oral book report, let Sal provide her with a 30-second introduction. If Marty is to read his poetry, Glenda can prepare the audience.

2) *Guests*. Included here are people from the community, other faculty members, and students from other classes. Topics might range from a science lecture to an illustrated travel talk.

3) *Films and other media*. For example, allow students to preview and introduce the filmstrips you use in science class. Or, before playing a tape of radio commercials that demonstrates the art of announcing, have a student tell the class what to listen for.

NAME _____

How to Put the Spotlight on Someone Else ⑩

Someday you may be asked to introduce a speaker. An introduction is a short speech that tells the audience who the main speaker is and what the speech will be about. Here's how to write an introduction.

Step 1. Before you write your introduction, have the speaker answer the following questions. Use more paper if necessary.

   A. What is the speaker's name and how is it pronounced?

     Speaker's name   It's pronounced

   B. What are several interesting facts about the speaker's job, hobbies, travels, skills, and so on?

   C. What is the title of the speech?

   D. What's the main idea?

   E. Why is the topic important?

Step 2. Use the information you gather to write your speech. Keep it short. Usually a one-minute introduction will be enough. You might begin with words like "Our speaker today is _____." End with, "And now let's welcome

57

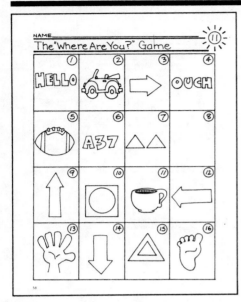

Listening Board Games

- giving directions
- following directions

The following activities are designed to sharpen the skills of giving and taking travel directions.

GRID-MAP GAME. Hand each student a copy of *Worksheet 11*, The "Where Are You?" Game. Whoever wants to play the leader writes a directions script:

1. Start at square A 37.
2. Move up one square.
3. Move right two squares and down three squares.
4. Move to the left until you come to a drawing that includes straight lines.

As the leader reads out the directions, listeners move a marker from place to place. After a set number of moves, the leader asks, "Where are you?" The answer will be a number in the upper-righthand corner of each square. (These grid numbers are not used when giving directions; that would make the game too easy.)

If you like drama, let everyone shout out the answer. If you like quiet, the leader can call on volunteers. If you like *more* quiet, the leader can simply say, "Raise your hand if you're on the such-and-such square." This may or may not be the right square!

Once students understand the game, they can create their own more elaborate game boards.

DEVELOPING DIRECTION-GIVING DEXTERITY. If someone has ever "helped" you to get lost by giving you crummy directions, you'll appreciate the importance of *Worksheet 12*, Helping People Get from Here to There. It gives students a chance to practice receiving and following directions based on a picture map. Because giving directions is tricky, you might guide the students through the game one time before they do it themselves. Explain the importance of using landmarks and of taking care when telling people to turn left or right.

As a critical reading challenge, you might create a set of directions purporting to guide someone from one place on the map to another. The directions should contain an error—for example, calling for a right turn when a left turn is required. The students' task is to locate and correct the error.

Worksheet 13, Giving Directions Using a Street Map, provides a more sophisticated version of the same activity. Later, students should practice their skills using a street map of your town.

Masks

- giving oral reports
- performing poetry

Masks, as the Greeks discovered several thousand years ago, have the power to *reveal* character as well as conceal it. If this is too highfalutin a rationale for having students don masks, here's something more down to earth: A simple mask can help shy kids stand before an audience with a fearless—if borrowed—face.

USING MASKS. Continue the ancient theatrical tradition of wearing masks to enliven plays and skits, be it *The Three Little Pigs* or *Julius Caesar*. But don't stop there. Why not have a child wear a monster mask when reading a monster poem or a cow mask when giving an oral report about farms?

FINDING AND CREATING MASKS. For starters, use *Worksheets 14—18*, Animal Masks, for presentations dealing with bears, birds, cats, dogs, or frogs. Kids can expand this gallery by drawing their own masks featuring other animals or even different types of creatures, such as robots and aliens from other planets.

For masks of celebrities, clip photographs from slick magazines such as *Time*, *Newsweek*, and *People*. Cover photos work especially well. Another possibility is writing directly to well-known personalities asking for 8 x 10 glossy photographs.

NAME _____
Bear Mask 14

Newsbriefs

- current events
- reading

The following short activity can have a big payoff in terms of current-events awareness.

STRAIGHT NEWS VERSION. A headline clipper—the teacher at first but students later on—clips a newspaper headine for each person in the room. The headlines, which should come from a single issue, should represent all types of news: local, national, international, economic, biographical, artistic, athletic, instructional, and so on. A few seconds are given for private rehearsal. Then the headline clipper signals each person in turn to read his or her headline. Designs for a microphone can be found on *Worksheet 19*.

MAP-ILLUSTRATION VERSION. The news reader starts off each report by locating the story on a map.

Off-the-Cuff Remarks

- thinking on one's feet
- giving an extemporaneous speech

The secret word for getting good at extemporaneous speaking is *practicepracticepractice*.

DEMONSTRATING OFF-THE-CUFF SPEAKING. Invite a facile speaker—perhaps someone who belongs to the International Toastmasters—to model extemporaneous speaking for your students. To maximize student involvement, have each one prepare a topic to toss at the guest.

PLAYING THE OFF-THE-CUFF SPEAKING GAME. You'll find two handouts designed to be clipped into individual "starter cards" for giving extemporaneous speeches: *Worksheet 20*, Off-the-Cuff Speaking from Pictures, and *Worksheet 21–22*, Off-the-Cuff Speaking from Word Scripts.

Pick out one of the cards and explain how it can be used to spark off countless speeches. For example, the "diamond ring" card could inspire one speaker to talk about how wonderful diamonds are while stimulating another to discuss the problems of poverty.

The basic way to use the materials is to set aside a special time for extemporaneous speeches. Right before speaking, each student will have about five seconds to study one of the cards clipped from *Worksheet 21* or *22*. The speaker will then talk extemporaneously for a set time—perhaps 30 seconds. (If you need more starter cards, have students create new ones using *Worksheets 21* and *22* as models.)

After students become comfortable talking off the cuff, you might try something more challenging: the *any time* extemporaneous speech. In this version, the students never know when they'll be handed a card and asked to talk. It could be right after recess, right before lunch, maybe in the middle of a math lesson. To avoid trauma, this game should include an "I pass" provision.

Finally, have students give extemporaneous speeches without using the starter cards. Always, however, give the speaker five seconds to choose a topic and to organize his or her thoughts.

One-Liners

- overcoming stage fright
- rehearsing

One example of good things coming in small packages is the one-liner appearing in such forms as:

exaggerations—My friends are so dumb they think being called stupid is a compliment.

daffynitions—Cauliflower: the main ingredient in dog biscuits

daffysayings—A rolling stone... can kill you.

These mini-jokes perfectly suit the classroom speech program for the following reasons: One, they take only a few seconds to tell, so stage fright hardly has time to happen. Two, their brevity makes it easy for even novices to hold the audience's attention. Three, they go by so fast every student can perform within a few minutes. Four, the format allows even unmotivated students to experience the power of repeated practice; it's no big chore to rehearse a three-second bit even 10 times.

WHOLE CLASS PERFORMANCES. Begin by posting the five rules of joke-telling:

1. Pick a joke *you* think is funny.
2. Rewrite the joke so it sounds like something you would say.
3. Memorize it.
4. Practice the joke by yourself until the words come out smoothly and easily.
5. When you practice in front of other people, don't laugh at the joke yourself. Let the audience do the laughing.

Next cut up *Worksheet 23*, One-Liners, and *Worksheet 24*, More One-Liners, and give each student a joke to rehearse. (To honor Rule #1 above, have on hand a supply of joke books for students who don't like the jokes they were assigned.)

Before the performance starts, establish an easy-to-follow order of presentation, for example, alphabetical order. This way the students will be able to pop up, one after the other, deliver the jokes, and sit back down.

INDIVIDUAL PERFORMANCES. Give students uncut copies of *Worksheets 23* and *24* so they can put together routines of half a dozen or more one-liners. (This material can be augmented with jokes taken from the humor books found in abundance in most libraries.)

NAME _____ 23

Oneliners

I know an artist who's so good that when he painted a mouse, his cat ate it.	Our neighbors are so stingy they charge themselves for rent.
The little strawberries were upset because their parents were in a jam.	I don't know how to drive a car, but if you want to drive a baby buggy, tickle its feet.
Our team played so badly even the other side was rooting for us.	This homework is so tough you could use it as a bullet-proof vest.
Humpty Dumpty had a terrible summer, but then he had a great fall.	It rained so hard yesterday people jumped into the lake to dry off.
My uncle is so tall he has to climb a ladder to shave himself.	Our pitcher throws balls so fast, batters have to start swinging two hours before the game starts.
A cookie jar is a "crummy" place to keep your money.	A bulldozer is what you call a bull when it's sleeping.
It was so hot yesterday even the sun went into the shade.	My dog is so mean he chased himself up a tree.

70

Overcoming *Um*

- giving a smooth delivery
- overcoming nervousness
- using silence

Remedies for overcoming *uh*s, *er*s, and *um*s are something like cures for hiccups. Everyone's got one but nobody's got much proof that it works. Over the long haul, experience usually does the trick. But in the meantime, if you want to know the author's "sure-fire" panaceas, read on.

ANTI-UM TECHNIQUE NUMBER ONE. Give students the following information: they don't have to fill every second of stage time with talk. People say things like *um* to buy time while trying to figure out what to say next. They could say nothing but they're afraid silence is "bad." It isn't. Most audience members would rather listen to the sound of grass growing than to be tortured by a string of empty *er*s.

ANTI-UM TECHNIQUE NUMBER TWO. Saying that speakers should say nothing is easier said than done. Keeping quiet requires practice. So, have each student stand up for a minute or two while saying *nothing*. Thinking, however, is permitted. (If this assignment makes individual performers too uncomfortable, begin by having students try it in groups of three or four.)

ANTI-UM TECHNIQUE NUMBER THREE. Each student gives an extemporaneous speech lasting about a minute. The student must pause for two seconds between each sentence to collect his or her thoughts but must not utter a single *uh*, *er* or *um*.

Panel Discussions

- listening
- thinking

Panels often are boring but they don't have to be. Groups can be fascinating to listen to as they share, argue, and collaborate. Done with pizzazz, a panel can turn out to be a heady, dramatic, and often fun experience. Think about:

a jury deliberating someone's fate

a group of astronauts, far out in space, trying to figure out why an engine won't start

the school board weighing the closing of one school versus another as a polarized community looks on

a team of doctors planning a heart transplant

So why then are classroom group discussions often less interesting than snail races? The answer is that producing a "good" panel discussion requires as much know-how, art, planning, and hard work as producing a "good" concert or play.

The effort to achieve mastery is worth it, however, since knowing how to participate on a panel is a lifelong citizenship and vocational skill.

STUDYING PANELS IN ACTION. The best way to introduce students to panels is to have them watch real panels in action. Here are some possibilities.

1. Invite a group of high school students (perhaps from the debate club) to stage a panel discussion in your room. Naturally, they should choose a topic of interest to your students, for example, "Is baseball a better sport than football?" or "Who's smarter—boys or girls?"

2. Arrange a field trip to a high school student council meeting, a school board meeting, or a city council meeting.

3. Ask students to watch one of those weekly televised discussion programs such as "Washington Week in Review."

4. Have your students reenact a panel by reading a transcript ordered from one of the shows mentioned in number 3, above. (If the reading level is too high, have older students or several of your colleagues do the performance.)

To get the most from these observations, have your students use *Worksheet 25*, Watching a Panel Meeting. This chart will help students focus on such group discussion skills as listening and asking questions.

STAGING PANELS. To produce a useful and interesting panel, the panel members must agree on these points: the purpose of the panel, the roles the members will play, the rules by which the panel will operate, and the necessary preparations.

Worksheet 26, Planning a Panel, gives students step-by-step directions for making sure all these tasks are accomplished. It also includes topic suggestions for the two basic kinds of panels—information sharing and decision making.

THINKING UP TOPICS FOR PANEL DISCUSSIONS. The most powerful topics will eventually come from the students' own lives. Use the following suggestions as models.

Information Sharing Panels

Members contribute facts, ideas, and opinions from varying perspectives. The more varied the points of view, the livelier the interaction and the more useful the product. Examples of information sharing panels are:

- "Joys of Collecting Things" (Panel members might include a stamp collector, a coin collector, a doll collector, a book collector.)
- "Fixing a 10-Speed Bike" (Each panel member handles a different part of the bike—tires, brakes, gears, and so on.)
- "What Makes Such-and-Such a Movie So Scary" (Each panelist covers a different aspect of the movie—music, sets, script, and so on.)
- "What are the Main Ideas in Such-and-Such a Book?"
- "Why Did Such-and-Such Current Event Happen?" (Each panelist presents a different theory.)
- "What We Learned from the Guest Speaker who Visited Us Yesterday" (This format can be used to review all sorts of shared experiences—field trips, movies, lectures, and so on.)

Decision Making Panels

Panelists go over the pros and cons of a decision and then take a vote.

- "Where Should the Class Picnic Be Held?"
- "Should the Driving Age Be Lowered to Ten Years?" (Many current issues being wrestled with by local, state, or national legislative groups can be studied in this lively way.)
- "Is Goldilocks Guilty of Breaking and Entering?"

Pantomime

- gesturing
- following a sequence
- overcoming stage fright

Pantomime can be an electrifying activity if students can find something to act out beyond a monkey eating a banana, and if students can learn how to break an action into its significant parts.

GIVING PANTOMIME STORY STARTERS. Use *Worksheets 27–29*, Pantomime Starters, to solve both of the problems mentioned above. These worksheets contain 16 cut-apart cards, each of which breaks an activity into four to six steps. The last step always asks students to think up a real ending for their performances.

INVENTING PANTOMIME STORY STARTERS. Provide *Worksheets 27–29* as models students can use to create their own pantomime story starters. Either the author or a classmate can perform the pantomime.

Play-by-Play Sportscasts

- oral reading
- modulating the voice

Sportscasting provides opportunities for incredibly colorful and dramatic oral descriptions: in football, a hundred yard runback of a kickoff; in baseball, a triple play; in tennis, a long rally; in track, a mile relay race; in daredevilry, the dive off a hundred-foot cliff. The task exercises such basic language skills as choosing details, sequencing events, modulating the voice, and timing.

The question is if you don't work for a radio or TV station, how do you get a chance to try sportscasting? *Worksheets 30 and 31* provide part of the answer.

DESCRIBING "PAPER" ACTION. Every sportscaster needs some action to describe. *Worksheet 30*, Here's the Pitch!, breaks a complicated baseball play into a series of pictures. Students name the players involved and then describe the action. *Worksheet 31*, New Sport, presents similar material, but with a fantasy game that requires inventing a new vocabulary.

These sportscasts can be performed "live" with the student using the microphone pictured on *Worksheet 19*. Another approach is to tape-record the descriptions.

NAME_____

Pantomime Starters (27)

Putting a worm on a fishing hook
1. Take the hook from the fishing tackle box.
2. Take the worm from the bait can.
3. Start putting the worm on the hook.
4. Make a face as if it's yucky to put the worm on the hook.
5. Make up an ending.

Zipping up a jacket
1. Put on a jacket.
2. Zip it part way up.
3. See that it's stuck.
4. Try to unstick the zipper.
5. Make up an ending.

Taking a splinter out
1. Look for the splinter in your finger.
2. Take a needle and hold it in a flame to kill the germs.
3. Try digging the splinter out with the needle.
4. Use your face to show it hurts.
5. Make up an ending.

Washing a window
1. Fill a bucket with water.
2. Pour in the soap.
3. Carry the bucket to the window.
4. Wash the window.
5. Dry the window.
6. Check the window for streaks.
7. Make up an ending.

Making toast
1. Get a slice of bread.
2. Put the bread in the toaster.
3. Wait for the bread to get toasted.
4. Put butter or jam on the toast.
5. Eat it.
6. Make up an ending.

Winning a prize
1. Get the mail from the mailbox.
2. Look through the letters.
3. Get excited by one letter.
4. Tear it open.
5. Read that you've just won a million dollars.
6. Make up an ending.

74

Poetry Reading

- developing an ear for the sound of language
- understanding poetry

Most poems are like songs. They were written to be performed rather than stored on paper. A powerful way to help children appreciate poetry is to stage frequent poetry readings—in class, for the whole school, and for the community at large.

INTRODUCING POETRY READINGS. Invite local poets from upper grades and from the community to read poetry in your school. To find poets, contact your town's librarian, local bookstore owners, and the sponsors of the high school poetry magazine or drama club.

HOLDING LIVE POETRY PERFORMANCES. The key to this activity is the *s* in *performances*. For real skill development, readings must be a frequent event. Consider holding readings once a week at lunch time. To win over the "I-hate-poetry crowd," plan a few special-interest readings. An entire 15-minute presentation might be devoted to a single genre, such as sports poetry, silly poetry, or science fiction poetry. (Yes, there is science fiction poetry. Flip the pages of the science fiction magazines found in many paperback bookstores.)

RECORDING POETRY PERFORMANCES. Try putting readings on tape. These tapes can be used as models for students in following classes. They can also be donated to the library. If you devoted an entire tape to the poems of a living poet, you might send a copy of the tape to that person for his or her reactions. Another outlet would be local radio stations which often wish to serve the community in some way.

PLAYING MUSIC WITH POETRY. An instrumental background can add drama and interest to a poetry reading. The music can be pre-recorded or it can be provided "live" by a teacher or student.

Pronunciation Presentations

- mastering tricky-to-pronounce words
- giving chalk talks
- involving an audience

With roughly a million words in our language, a pronunciation improvement program better not try to be exhaustive. The modest goal of the following activity is to build pronunciation confidence by having students master nearly three dozen pronunciation demons.

PRESENTING PRONUNCIATION CHALK TALKS. *Worksheets 32–34*, Pronunciation Chalk Talks, provides a month's worth of 60-second scripts dealing with such tricky-to-pronounce words as *library*, *herb*, and *pneumonia*. Each script starts with the parenthetical instruction to write the demon word on the chalkboard.

While the teacher will have to present the scripts for younger children, students reading at the fourth grade level should be able to handle the assignment themselves. This way they'll get the extra benefit of practicing such key speech skills as using the chalkboard and stimulating audience involvement. (A quick pre-presentation pronunciation check by the teacher is a good idea.)

CREATING PRONUNCIATION CHALK TALKS. Should you wish to continue the lessons, have your students use the worksheets as models for writing their own pronunciation scripts. These can focus on pronunciation demons collected from the daily newspaper, science magazines, menus of French restaurants, and daily conversations.

NAME _____ 32

Pronunciation Chalk Talks

(Write *Kansas* and *Arkansas* on the board.)

Sometimes two words look a lot alike but are said very differently. Take these two U. S. states. The first one is said "Kan zas." The second one is said "Ar kan saw." Say it with me: *Ar kan saw.*

(Write *athlete* on the board.)

People sometimes add an extra sound to a word. For example, they say *ath a leet.* The right way to say this word is *ath leet.* Say it with me: *ath leet.*

(Write *cafe* on the board.)

Some words are tricky to say because they come from foreign languages. For example, today's word—*ca fay,* which is a restaurant —comes from French. Say it with me: *ca fay.*

(Write *drowned* on the board.)

Some people add an extra *d* sound to this word making it *drownded.* The right way to say it is simply *drownd.* Say it with me: *drownd.*

(Write *colonel* on the board.)

Today's word, which names an officer in the armed forces, used to be spoken as it looks. But over the years people came to say it this way: *kernel,* just like a kernel of corn. Say it with me: *kernel.*

(Write *Connecticut* on the board.)

Today's word is an example of trouble caused by a silent letter. The name of this U. S. state is *Con e ti kut.* Try it with me: *Con e ti kut.*

(Write *debt* on the board.)

The letter *b* is not silent in many words, but it is in *debt* —pronounced *det*—which means something that is owed. Say it with me and I'll be in your *det.* Together now: *det.*

(Write *debut* on the board.)

When something first is seen, that's called its *day byoo.* If the word seems strange, that's because it comes directly from French and in the French language, very often the final *t* is silent. Try it with me now: *day byoo.*

79

Question and Answer Sessions

The worksheet on the left shows:

NAME_____ (35)
Question, Question, Who's Got a Question?

Learning how to ask good questions is an important skill. There are three main kinds of questions to know about.

1. A *yes/no* question gets a *yes* or *no* answer. An example is: "Can you count to ten?"
Write four questions that someone might ask you that you could answer with a *yes* or *no*.

2. A *short fact* question gets a short fact for an answer—usually a number or a name. An example is: "How many brothers do you have?" You might answer with the number fact "Three."
Write four questions that you could answer with a short fact.

3. An *open-ended* question is answered in a sentence or more. It could go on for pages and tell a long story. An example is: "How were you able to escape from the bear?" Of course, the person could answer in two words—"With luck." But the person asking the question really wants to hear the story.
Write four questions that would take you some time to answer.

- questioning
- listening
- thinking on one's feet

Answering questions from an audience is perhaps the most exciting part of public speaking. It can also be the scariest. The following exercises are meant to help students learn to face a *grilling* without getting burned.

ASKING QUESTIONS. Learning to *ask* good questions comes before learning to answer questions. *Worksheet 35*, Question, Question, Who's Got a Question?, covers the three main kinds of questions: yes/no, short answer, and open-ended.

ANSWERING SELF-GENERATED QUESTIONS. The rest of this section is based on the common-sense observation that it's easier to take a test if you know the questions ahead of time. Applying this to speechmaking, the speaker prepares to be questioned by asking questions first.

For a simple introduction to this I'll-answer-my-own-questions strategy, give students *Worksheet 36*, Press Conference. It's a role-playing activity in which the student, who has just won a million dollars, generates tough questions that a panel of reporters might ask. After writing their questions and answers, students in small groups can enact the press conferences.

For a slightly harder version of the same game, have each student write about 30 autobiographical questions, one for each member of the class. The questions can be about the speaker's hobbies, friends, travels, and so on. The members of the audience will then fire these prepared questions back at the person who wrote them.

Having gained some question-and-answer experience, each student can write a set of questions to be asked following an oral report. The presenter distributes the questions to the class, delivers the speech, and then calls on the audience members, who ask the ready-made questions. (This strategy is commonly used by television and radio talk show guests.) Finally, students prepare another speech, write questions based on it, but *do not* pass out the questions. They simply field questions from the audience. The final question is: what proportion of the questions were they able to anticipate?

Rating the Pros

- learning from professional speakers
- evaluating

Trying to select "the best" of anything is a task that exercises a person's critical faculties. But why let the folks who hand out Emmies and the Oscars have all the learning? Students can get into the act by awarding their own "Certificates of Excellence" to professional speakers and listeners, such as TV anchorpersons, radio talk show hosts, sportscasters, and other media pros.

PICKING THE WINNERS. Prepare a write-in-style ballot students will use to select favorite speakers in a variety of categories. The voting might take some time as students listen to "competing" DJs, weather reporters, newscasters, talk show hosts, comedians, and so on. For a more ambitious project, involve the entire school in the poll. In this case, assign one or two of your students to gather the votes from each room.

PRESENTING THE AWARDS. You and your students can personalize *Worksheet 37*, Certificate of Excellence, by writing in the name of your school and class, the name of the winner, and the name of the category. Besides mailing the certificates to the winners, you might also send a news release to the editor of your home-school newsletter and to the entertainment editor of your local newspaper.

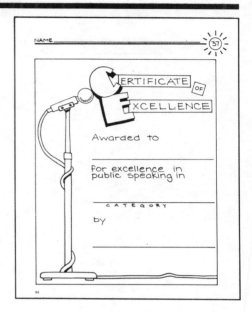

Reading an Audience

- overcoming stage fright
- making eye contact
- being an attentive audience member

Knowing how to read an audience is a crucial public-speaking skill. For one thing, it enables the speaker to find friendly, energy-giving faces. It also gives the speaker a chance to spot and deal with incipient problems such as confusion or boredom.

Worksheets 38–39, How to Read an Audience, picture the basic nonverbal clues audiences send speakers. The activity gives the student an initial practice in spotting audience members who are bored, confused, surprised, and so on.

Repeat After Me

- listening
- memorizing

For sheer drama, few speaking and listening activities can match swearing an oath of office or taking a formal vow.

RECITING FAMOUS OATHS. One need not actually win an election, get married, or join a club in order to take an oath. Using *Worksheet 40*, Repeat After Me, you can simulate the experience in your classroom. The teacher or a student simply reads one of the texts phrase by phrase. A small group of students—or the entire class—listens carefully and then repeats the words.

COLLECTING OATHS. Have students collect oaths by writing to members of the armed forces, local and national government officials, doctors and members of other professional groups, and members of clubs. The class can then practice reciting these oaths.

CREATING OATHS. Students can use the examples they collect as models for creating original oaths for individuals such as robots, time travelers, magicians, and the like. These new oaths can extend the oath-taking activity described above.

Saying a Song

- reading with expression
- listening to lyrics

Whining guitars and thundering drums make it hard to understand, let alone appreciate, most pop lyrics. That's a shame. A surprising number of these songs can serve as high-motivation models for teaching such topics as metaphor, descriptive writing, and storytelling. An even better use of this material is in developing listening and speaking skills.

LISTENING TO LYRICS. Simply playing a record and having kids snap their fingers won't due. To focus the ear, the teacher must specify particular items to listen for. Possibilities include colorful adjectives, figures of speech, or unusual points of view.

SAYING SONG LYRICS. You don't have to be Frank Sinatra or Carole King to interpret song lyrics. Thoughtful reading is all it takes. Here's the set-up: A student or a small group of students reads—with feeling—the lyrics of a hit song. When the reading is finished, the audience listens to the lyrics as performed on the record. The whole group might then do a sing-along. (This activity may not sound like much on paper but it can be amazingly dramatic in the classroom.)

FINDING LYRICS TO PERFORM. It's impossible for an outsider to suggest suitable song lyrics for your classroom. Tastes vary; there are so many kinds of pop music (easy rock, country and western, folk, and so on). Levels vary; what's appropriate for second graders may have no value for older kids. Times vary; new songs appear weekly. Uses vary; a lyric that's powerful for teaching metaphor may have lousy rhymes.

So how do you pick the material? One way is to invest a few hours listening to the radio with a notebook close by. Jot down songs whose lyrics a) touch you; b) can be understood by your students; c) incorporate devices and skills you want to cover, such as descriptive writing or story structure; and d) reflect the quality of usage you want students to strive for. Older students can assist in this quest once they understand the criteria listed above.

While you can always go out and buy sheet music, a better option is to have students transcribe the words from a recording. Transcribing provides excellent practice in careful listening, spelling, and punctuation.

Show and Tell

- illustrating a speech
- speaking extemporaneously

Show and Tell not only provides low-pressure speech-making practice; it's also *the* model for all effective communication. When you see kids filling their papers with mumbo jumbo, remind them that writing is merely Show and Tell on paper. Clear talk counts.

The trouble is that many kids can't find subjects to present though they have the whole world to draw upon. But maybe having the whole world is overwhelming. One solution is to create categories that force children to focus. Here are some examples:

ORDINARY OBJECTS. The speaker gives a detailed, eye-opening description of an object that most people look at but never *see*: a penny or any other coin, a dollar bill (how many *one*'s are printed on it?), a safety pin, a T-shirt, a chalkboard eraser, a pencil, a ballpoint pen, a postage stamp, and so on.

NOISY SUBJECTS. The speaker collects a few of one thing—pennies, checkers, thimbles, bottle caps, plastic spoons, keys, combination locks, and so on. After hearing the objects shaken inside a coffee can, the audience can ask 20 questions to identify them. Limit random guessing by requiring that the first 10 questions be fact oriented: "Is it used in a sport?" "Can you buy one in a bakery?" "Is it for pets?"

EDIBLE SUBJECTS. Each speaker is assigned a different food. Some reports can help people better understand such everyday foods as oranges, eggs, or walnuts. Other reports might introduce more exotic foods, such as kiwi, uglifruit, and escargot.

COLORFUL SUBJECTS. On a given day all students present an object with the same color.

TOO-BIG-TO-BRING-IN SUBJECTS. Show-and-Tell reporters describe large objects they have seen firsthand—airplanes, skyscrapers, buses, billboards, and so on.

ALPHABETICAL SUBJECTS. Ask each student to bring in and share an object that starts with an assigned letter of the alphabet.

Sound-Effects Stories

- listening
- oral reading
- writing

Inside most kids are *varooooooms*, *oinnnnks*, *zaaaaps*, and all sorts of other expressive noises waiting to be unleashed. This activity has students convert their natural onomatopoeic talents into artful sound effects that can add humor or drama to read-aloud stories. Students make the sound effects when their sound occurs in the story.

PRACTICING SOUND EFFECTS. A major theme of this book is that every performance should be rehearsed —even an *achooo* or a *ding-dong*. Therefore, before trying a sound-effects story, have students practice the sound effects on *Worksheet 41*, Object Sound Cards, and *Worksheet 42*, Animal Sound Cards.

To overcome shyness and embarrassment, perform each sheet as a whole-class choral reading. Later, encourage solo sneezes, squeaks, and so on. (For tips on more accurate imitations of natural sounds, see the Animal Voices activity.)

Notice that *Worksheets 41* and *42* each contain one weird-looking noise-maker—a Rube-Goldberg-like gadget in the first case, and a fantasy animal in the other. Creating sounds for these two items will give someone's vocal imagination a real workout.

PERFORMING NOISY WORKS. To start, you'll need onomatopoeia-rich sentences, stories, poems, or essays. You can write them yourself but, if your students are able, let them turn out texts (or adapt fairy tales) that feature some—or all—of the sounds pictured on *Worksheets 41* and *42*. The writing should proceed as normal except that the word *sound* should be inserted following each *roar*, *moo*, or other noise. For example:

> It was around three in the morning when the phone (sound) rang. I turned on the light (sound), marched to the kitchen (sound), and answered the phone. At the other end was a rooster (sound).

Cut out sound cards and distribute to students. When they hear their sound mentioned in the story, they make the sound.

P.S. If your students are too young to write noisy material, "hire" older students as writers. For a sample of a student work, see *Worksheet 43*, A Sound-Effects Story.

Sound Punctuation

- punctuating
- playing with the voice

Back in the 1950s comedian Victor Borge invented "sound punctuation," proving yet again that *everything* is potentially funny, even commas and periods.

The routine is simple. First, invent a nonsense sound for each punctuation mark. The funnier the sounds, the better. For example:

    period = pooot
    question mark = zee-yin pooot
    comma = ffpp
    quotation mark = krip
    exclamation point = blam pooot

Then, while reading aloud any passage, make the sound of each punctuation mark encountered *pooot* (.)

INTRODUCING SOUND PUNCTUATION. It would be ideal if you could demonstrate the activity by playing Borge's Columbia album, *Caught in the Act*. Alas, the record is no longer in print, but you might find a copy at a used-record store. As an alternative, replicate the skit using local talent: an actor from the high school drama club, one of your students, or how about doing it yourself *zee-yin pooot* (?)

FINDING SCRIPTS. Any punctuation-rich passage will do. Try using familiar material such as paragraphs from a textbook or even the school rules handbook.

Speaking of Speakers and Listeners

- interviewing
- oral reporting

It isn't only actors, disc jockeys, and other performers who need to be good at speaking and listening. Oral language plays an important role in many fields. Learning about the less obvious uses of these skills can prove motivating to students who are not Broadway bound.

FIGURING OUT WHO'S TALKING AND LISTENING. Students can fill in *Worksheet 44*, Talking and Listening on the Job, as the starting point for a class discussion on oral language as a vocational skill.

Speech! Speech!

- planning a formal speech
- rehearsing a speech
- evaluating a speech

This activity covers techniques used in "prepared" speeches: the oral report (lecture), the how-to-do-it demonstration, the illustrated talk, and the introduction.

INTRODUCING THE BASICS OF SPEECHMAKING. Giving a formal speech is a complex activity that includes such steps as generating ideas, researching, rehearsing, delivering the words, and evaluating. The best way to teach this process is to have an experienced speaker give your class a how-to-do-it speech about speechmaking. Sources of such speakers are the local toastmaster club, the high school speech club, City Hall, radio and TV stations, or local businesses.

The second-best way to cover the basics is to give students *Worksheet 45*, The Speech Game. This fill-in recipe in game-board form can be used again and again with each new speech assignment.

To help students understand each step, the teacher should go through the recipe, perhaps displaying the worksheet with an overhead projector. You may wish to discuss each of the steps in some length, especially number 4, research, which is not dealt with as a separate topic in this book. The main point to make about gathering information is that books aren't the only source. The liveliest presentations often include information gained by interviewing experts and by making eyewitness observations.

BREAKING A SUBJECT INTO SMALLER, MANAGEABLE PARTS. The key step in planning a speech is dividing the main topic into subtopics. *Worksheet 46*, Breaking a Subject into Pieces, gives students practice in this tricky but learnable skill.

REHEARSING A SPEECH. It's one thing to tell students that they *should* rehearse their speeches. It's another thing to give them a structure for carrying out the practice. Enter *Worksheet 47*, How to Rehearse a Speech. This reusable handout includes rehearsing alone and with a trial audience.

EVALUATING A SPEECH. Performance without evaluation leads nowhere. By providing the class with *Worksheet 48*, Speech Review Checklist, you can stimulate genuinely helpful peer evaluation.

Speechless "Speeches"

- making eye contact
- practicing good posture
- overcoming stage fright

Experts agree that eye contact forges a powerful link between speaker and audience. But looking people in the eye can be tough, especially when there are dozens or hundreds of eyes to deal with. The following activities are meant to make the job easier by allowing novices to *focus* on focusing.

EASY VERSION. The speaker strides confidently to the front of the room, gets set, looks three or four people in the eye, gives a "thank you" nod, and exits cleanly.

CHALLENGING VERSION. In almost every audience will be one or a few souls willing to root for the speaker. Knowing how to spot and link up with them is an invaluable speaking skill. Here's how to practice it.

While the speaker is out of the room, pick three members of the audience who will wear friendly, encouraging expressions. Everyone else will look bored or angry.

Now, call the speaker in. He or she will give another wordless speech only this time the task is to scan the room and locate the three "allies." After giving them some nonverbal acknowledgement, the speaker sits down. Afterward, the presenter identifies by name the three friends in the audience.

FOLLOW-UP REPORT. Have each student report on a professional speaker's use of eye contact. Students can use live specimens: teachers, guest lecturers, and door-to-door salespeople. But don't overlook the vast pool of televised talkers: newscasters, sportscasters, weather persons, announcers in commercials (especially low-budget car and furniture ads on non-network stations), video ministers, and teachers on educational programs.

The report should name the speaker, explain what the speech was about (news, dog food, the weather, and so on), tell where the speaker looked most of the time (at the audience, at the speech script, at the ground, somewhere else). Older students can give a more precise report by using a stopwatch to time the quantity of eye contact.

Story Hour

- reading a text
- using props
- overcoming stage fright

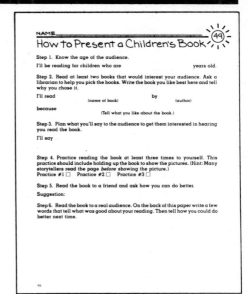

Why let the librarians have all the fun? Students at every grade level can—and should—present literature to younger students.

The works of Dr. Seuss, Margaret Brown, and Steven Kellogg will challenge the reading skills of your most sophisticated students. Sixth graders who learn how to squeeze the last drop of drama out of *Peter Rabbit* are preparing themselves for confronting all the masterworks—*Hamlet* included.

But what about first graders who are just learning to read? They can be equally involved by entertaining kindergartners with the actions and characters found in wordless picture books.

INTRODUCING STORYTELLING. Being in the audience at a story hour is one thing. Actively observing the storyteller in order to pick up on his or her tricks is something else. Arrange for your students to watch the school or town librarian read and tell stories. Before the "show," go over *Worksheet 49*, How to Present a Children's Story. It will help your novice storytellers know what to look for. Of great value would be a follow-up question-and-answer session during which students could query the storyteller about such issues as picking a book to read, working up an introduction, rehearsing, using visuals, and involving the audience.

REHEARSING STORY HOUR PRESENTATIONS. Before working with authentic audiences, have your students put on practice story hours in your room. Students can use *Worksheet 49* to guide them in preparing to present a book. In addition, these presentations might include stories told in the storyteller's words; sing-alongs; puppets telling stories or reciting poems; and even small-scale circus acts, such as magic tricks or juggling.

PUTTING ON STORY HOURS. Consider offering a weekly story hour that can be held in the library, the auditorium, or the classrooms of the younger students. (Of course, the story hour need not be a full 60 minutes. For very young children, 15 minutes should suffice. That would be long enough for your students to deliver the text of two short books and maybe a couple of poems.)

Telephone Calls

- using the telephone
- writing scripts

It's been over a century since Alexander Graham Bell placed that first phone call, yet many folks are still wary of the invention. The following activities aim to help students feel more comfortable and confident when it comes to "reaching out and touching someone" electronically.

WRITING TELEPHONE SCRIPTS. One way to overcome fear of phoning is to write out the script for a phone call before picking up the receiver. *Worksheet 50,* Telephone Calling Scripts, are "speech starters" for such basic types of calls as making an appointment, shopping, and handling an emergency.

REHEARSING TELEPHONE CALLS. Students should practice telephoning using their scripts as starting points for pretend conversations. (Nonreaders can improvise on the topics.) Set the stage by having telephone partners sit back-to-back. For greater realism, use inexpensive walkie-talkies. These will permit your phony phoners to sit far apart or even in different rooms.

CALLING FOR REAL. After students have written and rehearsed telephone scripts, encourage them to use their skills in the real world. You might suggest to parents that they assign children such phone chores as ordering take-out pizzas, finding out when movies start, ordering tickets for concerts, and so on.

MAKING ONE-SIDED PHONE CALLS. Have students act out one side of a phone conversation. It can be something serious (a call to the fire department), something dramatic (a call to the president or the prime minister), or something silly (a comical call to Superman or Charlie Brown).

Testing! Testing!

- using the microphone
- speaking clearly

If you've ever felt awkward when addressing a group through a microphone, there's a simple reason: Using a microphone is not a natural way to get words across. TV reporters or rock musicians can make it seem easy because they constantly practice. Too often kids practice at the worst possible time: when delivering a real speech.

PRACTICING WITH THE MICROPHONE. Mastering the microphone is like mastering a musical instrument: progress comes only with regular practice. In your classroom try installing a microphone that students can use on a daily basis for making announcements, reading oral reports, and so on. If you can't get a working mike, make one! *Worksheet 19* describes how. Even a cardboard microphone will help students get used to talking with a device in front of them.

DEVELOPING MICROPHONE MANNERS. Here are some tips for using a microphone:

Tip 1. Set up the microphone and amplifier BEFORE the audience arrives. Test it and make any changes that are needed.

Tip 2. Make sure the speaker is closer to the audience than the microphone is. Otherwise, a squealing noise may come out of the speaker.

Tip 3. Put the microphone at mouth level so you don't have to stand on your toes or bend over. Usually there's a simple way to move the microphone up or down.

Tip 4. Keep your mouth about a hand's width from the microphone. This is about three inches—seven centimeters. If your mouth is too close to the microphone, your words may come out unclear. If your mouth is too far away, the audience may not hear you.

Tip 5. Speak in a normal voice. Don't shout or whisper.

Tip 6. Do NOT touch the microphone while you're speaking. If you do touch it, you will make unpleasant noises.

Tip 7. Keep your mouth pointed toward the microphone. If you move your mouth from side to side, your voice will sometimes be loud and sometimes soft.

Tongue (Un)Twisters

- articulating
- listening
- memorizing
- writing sentences

Articulation exercises will not, by themselves, convert sloppy speakers into exacting enunciators. Still, tongue-testing, lip-laboring, jaw-jolting mini-speeches can at least initiate interest in careful word formation.

But watch out! Just as driving too fast can ruin a car, racing through tongue twisters can cause articulation catastrophies. Students should say the words no faster than correct enunciation permits. The goal is to *un*twist, rather than tangle, the tongue.

UNTWISTING TOGETHER. Each student will rehearse and then present a tongue twister clipped from *Worksheet 51*, Tongue Twisters. After this solo performance, which might involve displaying an illustration of the tongue twister, the leader will guide the whole class through the material several times. The tempo should be molasses-like slow the first time, then faster on each succeeding repetition.

CREATING TONGUE (UN)TWISTERS IN THREE EASY STEPS. Lest you run out of tongue twisters, here's a recipe for having students create their own. Eventually, these can be shared orally with other classes, turned into illustrated books, distributed on tape to kids in other schools, or used in tongue-twister competitions.

The first step in inventing a tongue twister is to choose a pair of almost-alike "key sounds," such as the *s* and *sh* in "She sells seashells by the seashore."

Step two requires collecting words that contain these sounds. For example, suppose you wanted to create a tongue twister using *fl* and *fr* sounds. Your initial word collections might be:

fl—flip, flood, floor, flea, flat
fr—friend, fried, frozen

In step three you form a phrase or sentence using some of the collected words. For best results, the key sounds should alternate—*fr* word, then *fl* word, and so on. Since the tongue twister should make some sort of sense, you may have to add new words to the original stock. With a little rearranging and editing, voila:

Fred flipped frozen flapjacks.

Vocal Variety

- creating characters
- varying volume, pace, and emphasis

These vocal variety activities are dedicated to Mel Blank, the "invisible" actor who created voices of many cartoon personalities including Bugs Bunny.

CREATING VOICES. *Worksheet 52*, Look Who's Talking, presents four characters with empty dialogue balloons. Have each student write identical words in the balloon—"I'm hungry" will work fine—and then invent distinctive voices for each character. The student will then perform the parts for a listener who will try to match the voices with the pictures. (Provide additional copies of the worksheet so that students can experiment with different dialogue. They can further extend the activity by drawing and performing other characters.)

UNPACKAGING VOCAL VARIETY. Collect tin-can and candy labels, newspaper and magazine ads, junk-mail brochures, travel flyers and other materials on which words are printed in varying sizes.

The simplest way to turn this *typographical* variety into *vocal* variety is to have students read the large-size words loudly and the small-size words softly.

INTERPRETING SERIOUS MATERIAL. Once students get the hang of vocal variety, let them hone their skills on more traditional material. For starters, write a short sentence several times on the board. Capitalize a different word each time:

> THE lunchroom is noisy.
> The LUNCHROOM is noisy.
> The lunchroom IS noisy.
> The lunchroom is NOISY.

Lead the class in an oral reading of the sentences, emphasizing the capitalized word each time. Discuss which version makes the most sense.

Have each student repeat the activity using a found or original sentence. The presentations can be done in small groups or in front of the whole room.

Finally, students should choose material for a one-minute reading: a poem, an ad, or an excerpt from a longer piece. The task is to underline the key word or words in each sentence and then read the material giving emphasis where it's due.

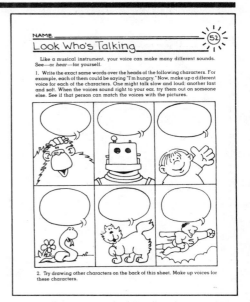

NAME_____
Look Who's Talking — (52)

Like a musical instrument, your voice can make many different sounds. See—or *hear*—for yourself.

1. Write the exact same words over the heads of the following characters. For example, each of them could be saying "I'm hungry." Now, make up a different voice for each of the characters. One might talk slow and loud; another fast and soft. When the voices sound right to your ear, try them out on someone else. See if that person can match the voices with the pictures.

2. Try drawing other characters on the back of this sheet. Make up voices for these characters.

Weather Reports

- observing
- science reporting
- using puppets

Weather reporters may be hated and blamed but they're seldom ignored. That's what makes weather reporting such a plum of a speech assignment. Here are suggestions for implementing a daily classroom, or even school-wide, weather report.

STUDYING THE COMPETITION. Exactly what does the TV weatherman or weatherwoman do? *Worksheet 53*, Report on the Weather Reporter, helps students analyze the job in preparation for doing it themselves.

GATHERING THE WEATHER DATA. Every weather reporter needs facts as well as hunches. The easiest way for your students to gather information about temperature, cloudiness, wind velocity, precipitation, and so on is to clip reports from the daily newspaper, listen to the hourly radio news, or phone the local weather service number.

For much more fun, however, set up a classroom weather station. It might include:

- a thermometer fixed outside your window
- a map, with a transparent plastic sheet for tracing storm movements
- a barometer
- a rain guage
- a wind-direction indicator

PRESENTING THE WEATHER. Each day you can have a different student deliver the weather. For a change of pace, consider having the reports put on as mini-puppet shows. Simply clip apart *Worksheet 54*, Weather Puppets. Students can use these puppets on their fingers or mount them on sticks.

Word-of-the-Day Listening Game

- listening
- developing vocabulary

This activity was inspired by the old Groucho Marx "Say-the-secret-word-and-receive-a-hundred-dollars" routine. Instead of a duck, there's a bunch of ears.

CLASSROOM VERSION. At the start of the day, the teacher writes the "magic" word of the day on the board and explains what it means. The word can be from a vocabulary development book, from the spelling list, from the daily newspaper, from a novel, from an advertisement, from anywhere. At least occasionally it should be a word that's new to most of the students.

The teacher uses the word several times during the day. Whenever a student hears it, he or she holds up the "I heard the word" ear for everyone to see. When called on, the student echoes the teacher's sentence. The entire class should be encouraged to use the word at least once before the end of the day. (All the "ears" you need can be made from *Worksheet 55*, Ear It Is.)

SCHOOL-WIDE VERSION. The word is announced to the entire school community either over the PA as part of the morning announcements or via a word-of-the-day bulletin board (see the bulletin board section).

WORKSHEETS

Boarding Passes

flight #235 London Row 1 C	flight #238 Rome Row 1 C	flight #128 Mexico City Row 1 F
flight #235 London Row 2 B	flight #238 Rome Row 2 D	flight #128 Mexico City Row 2 A
flight #235 London Row 4 G	flight #238 Rome Row 3 E X	flight #128 Mexico City Row 3 G
flight #235 London Row 10 D X	flight #238 Rome Row 12 F	flight #128 Mexico City Row 11 B
flight #235 London Row 12 A	flight #238 Athens Row 14 G	flight #128 Mexico City Row 14 G X
flight #235 London Row 17 J	flight #238 Athens Row 15 A X	flight #128 Mexico City Row 17 J
flight #235 London Row 20 H	flight #238 Athens Row 17 B	flight #128 Mexico City Row 19 E
flight #235 London Row 21 H X	flight #238 Athens Row 19 H	flight #128 Mexico City Row 21 F
flight #235 London Row 22 B	flight #238 Athens Row 20 C X	flight #128 Lima Row 22 D X
flight #235 London Row 24 F X	flight #238 Athens Row 24 A	flight #128 Lima Row 24 A X

Boarding Announcement Script ②

Announcer #1: Welcome to gate area 5. There will be three flights leaving from this area today. Please check your tickets carefully. Flight 235 for London will board through Gate 5A.

Announcer #2: Flight 238 for Rome and Athens will board through Gate 5B.

Announcer #3: Flight 128 for Mexico City and Lima will board through Gate 5C.

Announcer #1: May I have your attention please. Will all passengers scheduled on flight 235 please raise their hands. (Wait until you see hands.) Thanks. Hands down. We will start boarding in a moment.

Announcer #2: Attention. May I see the hands of those people scheduled on flight 238? (Wait until you see hands.) Thank you. You may lower your hands. We will start boarding in a minute.

Announcer #3: Now hear this. Passengers on flight #128 do not raise your hands. (If someone raises a hand, repeat the direction.)

Announcer #1: May I see the hands of passengers boarding through Gate 5A? Thank you.

Announcer #2: If you're going to board through Gate 5B, please raise your left hand. Thank you.

Announcer #3: If your gate is 5C, raise both hands.

Announcer #1: We will be boarding flight #235 by row numbers. May I see the hands of those passengers seated in rows 1 through 10? Fine.

Announcer #2: On flight 238, may I see the hands of passengers seated in rows 17 through 24? Very good.

Announcer #3: On flight 128, may I see the hands of passengers seated in rows 1 through 3 and 21 through 24?

Announcer #1: We are now about to start boarding flight 235. If you have a ticket with an X, please wait until called. Now, all passengers on flight 235 in rows 17 through 24 may step forward and give your tickets to the attendant at Gate 5A.

Announcer #2: (Wait until everyone is seated.) All passengers on flight #238 who are going to Athens and who have an X on their ticket may now walk to Gate 5B.

Announcer #3: (Wait until everyone is seated.) All passengers in rows 1 through 14 on flight 128 may board through Gate 5C.

Announcer #2: All passengers on flight 235 who have an X on their ticket may now board through Gate 5A.

Announcer #2: All passengers heading for Rome may now board.

Announcer #3: All passengers on flight 128 who still haven't boarded may now board.

Announcer #1: All passengers on flight 235 may board.

SYMBOLS FOR CHARADES

 Book: Hands form an open book.

 T.V. Show: Draw a box in the air to show a T.V. screen.

 Play: Take a bow.

Song: Put hands on both sides of mouth.

 Sounds like: Cup hand next to ear.

 Little word: Hold thumb and index finger an inch apart.

 Number of syllables: Place fingers on your arm to show the number of syllables in a word, then which syllable.

 Number of words: Hold up fingers to show the number of words in your challenge, then which word.

 Longer version of the word: Draw your hands apart as if pulling taffy.

 Shorter version of the word: Make a chopping motion with one hand on the other.

Here's What I Heard

How many of these sounds do you notice every day? Here's your chance to find out. In the spaces below, list the sounds you hear during the next 24 hours.

Musical Instruments: List all you hear—piano, guitar, drums, flute, trumpet, and so on. You can list those you hear live as well as those heard on recordings.

Music: List all the different kinds of music you hear—rock and roll, classical, country and western, jazz, and so on.

Noises: List animal sounds, weather sounds, machine sounds, and so on.

Voices: List all kinds—angry, friendly, scared, old, young, and so on.

Talk: List the ways you hear people using talk—to ask questions, teach, argue, buy, tell stories, give news, and so on.

News Scenes

Incredible News Scene

Guided Art Designs

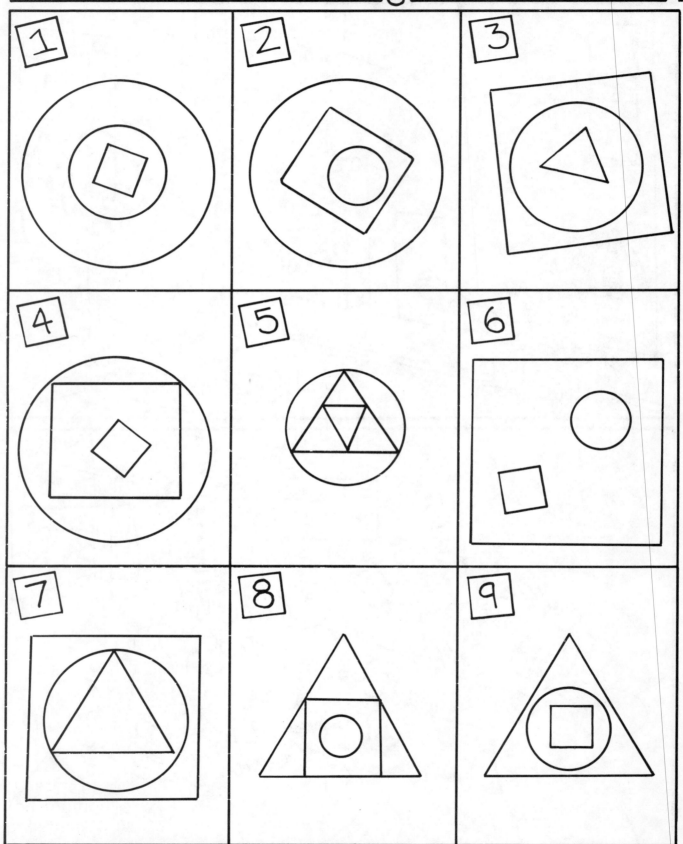

How To Make a Peanut Butter Sandwich

1. Study the pictures below. Pick out only four of them that you will use to show how to make a peanut butter sandwich. Cut out these four pictures, put them in the right order, and paste them onto another sheet of paper. Under each picture, write a sentence that tells what the step is all about.

2. Pick any simple skill you know how to do. It can be frying an egg, tying a shoelace, making a paper airplane, or anything. Draw four to six pictures that show how to do it. Put these pictures on a sheet of paper and write a sentence under each one that explains the picture.

How to Teach People to Do Anything

Here's a plan to follow when you want to teach an audience how to juggle, how to whistle, how to play a game, how to make a paper airplane, how to eat with chopsticks, or how to do any skill that you're good at.

Step 1. Name the skill you want to teach. _____

Step 2. List the materials you'll need to teach the skill. (For example, to teach jump rope tricks you'd need a jump rope.)

_____

_____

Step 3. Break the lesson into important parts and list them in order.

    First I'll _____

    Second I'll _____

    Third I'll _____
    (If you need more room, use the back.)

Step 4. Practice the steps by yourself. Decide what words and actions you'll use to make each step as clear as possible.

Step 5. Teach the skill to a trial audience. Ask for suggestions that will make your presentation clearer.

_____

_____

Step 6. Teach the skill to your real audience.

Step 7. Write what you liked about the way you taught the lesson.

_____

Step 8. Write how the lesson could have been clearer or more interesting.

_____

How to Put the Spotlight on Someone Else

Someday you may be asked to introduce a speaker. An introduction is a short speech that tells the audience who the main speaker is and what the speech will be about. Here's how to write an introduction.

Step 1. Before you write your introduction, have the speaker answer the following questions. Use more paper if necessary.

    A. What is the speaker's name and how is it pronounced?

        Speaker's name _____ It's pronounced _____

    B. What are several interesting facts about the speaker's job, hobbies, travels, skills, and so on?

        _____

    C. What is the title of the speech? _____

    D. What's the main idea? _____

    E. Why is the topic important? _____

        _____

        _____

Step 2. Use the information you gather to write your speech. Keep it short. Usually a one-minute introduction will be enough. You might begin with words like "Our speaker today is _____ ." End with, "And now let's welcome _____ ."

NAME _____

The "Where Are You?" Game

Helping People Get from Here to There

Helping people find their way from one place to another is not easy. Here's a chance for you to practice this important skill.

Step 1. Pick a starting place on the map below. It can be the fountain, the forest, the haunted house, or anywhere.

Step 2. Pick an ending place on another part of the map.

Step 3. On another piece of paper, write directions for getting from the starting place to the ending place. Give *landmarks* along the way. For example, you might write, "Go past the cemetery." Be extra careful when telling people whether to turn left or right.

Step 4. When you're done, give the map to someone, but don't tell the person the ending place. Just read your directions aloud and see if the listener ends up at the right place. If he or she doesn't, try to figure out what went wrong.

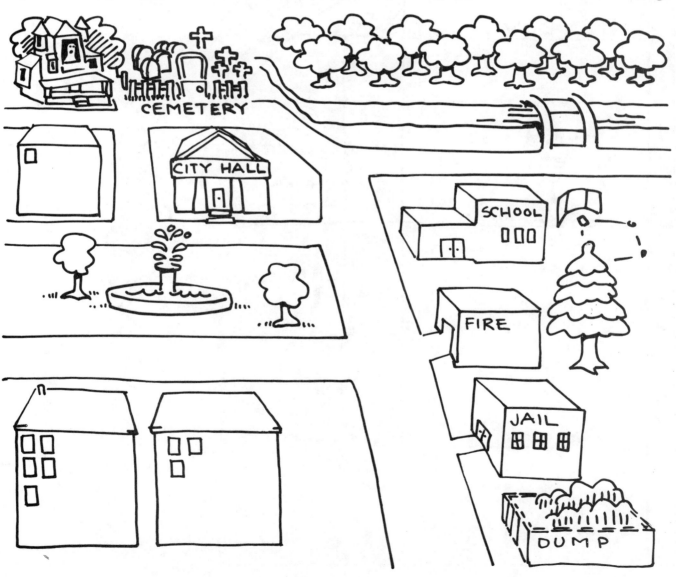

Giving Directions Using a Street Map

Pick a starting and an ending point on the map below. On a separate piece of paper, write a set of directions that tell how to get from the first place to the second. When you're done writing, give the map to someone and read your directions. See if the person gets to the place you had in mind. If he or she doesn't, try to figure out what went wrong.

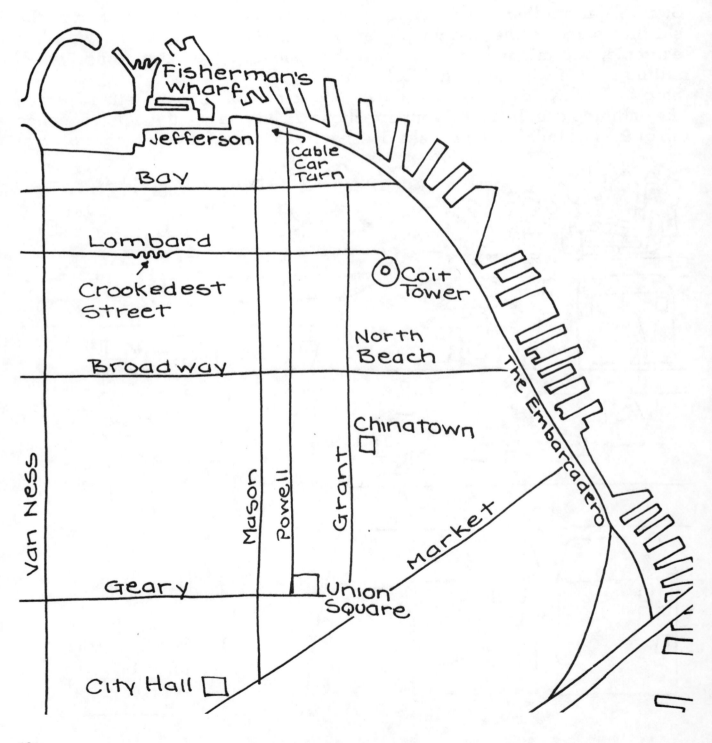

Bear Mask

Cat Mask

Dog Mask

Duck Mask

Frog Mask

Make a Mike

Materials: cardboard tube from roll of toilet paper; styrofoam ball of the same diameter; long poking tool, such as a knitting needle; long length of cord; masking tape or cloth tape; silver spray paint; black construction paper; paste.

1. Poke a hole through the diameter of the styrofoam ball about a third of the way down. Insert the length of cord (you might need to use the poking tool to push through the cord) and tie it as shown.

2. Insert the styrofoam ball in the top of the cardboard tube with the cord dangling down through the tube. The ball should sit snugly. If necessary wrap some tape around its diameter to make a closer fit.

3. Secure the styrofoam ball in place in the cardboard tube by wrapping a piece of tape around that overlaps the top edge of the tube and the middle of the ball.

4. Paint the top half of the construction silver.

5. Cover the tube itself with black construction paper.

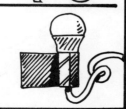

Off-The-Cuff Speaking From Pictures

Off-the-Cuff Speaking from Words

You find yourself stuck with the three little pigs while the wolf is threatening to blow the house down.
> What do you say to the pigs?
> What do you say to the wolf?

You pick up the telephone and a creature from another planet tells you that it plans to blow up the Earth. How do you get the creature to change its mind?

You've been chosen to be the first person to travel back in time.
> Why were *you* chosen?
> Where will you go in time?
> Who will you visit?

You have just returned from a visit to the future.
> What's the most amazing thing you saw?
> Would you go back?
> Explain your answer.

Someone hands you a microphone and tells you that everyone in the world can hear and understand you. What do you say?

You have just won an elephant in a TV contest.
> How do you feel?
> What are you going to do with the elephant?

You're a barber. For a few seconds you weren't paying attention and you cut too much from someone's hair. What do you say?

You're a football coach and your team is losing by 100 points. Thirty minutes are left in the game. What do you tell your players?

You are the first dog to learn how to talk to human beings. What do you have to say?

You are the first tree to learn how to talk to human beings. What do you have to say?

You have just lost the election for mayor in your town. The radio and TV stations want you to say a few words. What do you say?

You've invented a way to read other people's minds.
> What's good about being able to do this?
> What's not so good?

Off-the-Cuff Speaking from Words

Your best friend borrowed a lot of money from you and promised to repay it in a week. It's two months later and you meet your friend who still hasn't paid you a penny. What do you say?

You open up a newspaper and see your picture on page one. The story says you robbed a bank yesterday though, in fact, you were out of town. You call up the newspaper. What do you say?

You borrowed a lot of money from your best friend and promised to repay it in a week. It's two months later and your friend calls to ask for the money. What do you say?

You're flying in a small airplane when the pilot suddenly gets sick and faints. You have no idea how to fly a plane but you do get the radio to work. What do you say?

You're the best hitter on your baseball team but you just struck out to lose the biggest game of the year. What do you tell your teammates?

You wake up and find that you have become invisible. The phone rings and your best friend is on the line. What do you say?

You're the first person to have a brain transplant. The doctors put your brain into the body of a lion. What do you tell people when they meet you?

You have just been elected leader of the country. It's time to give your victory speech. What do you have to say?

You're a door-to-door seller of smoke alarms. What do you tell people when they open the door?

You meet someone who has never heard of television. How do you explain what it is?

You get to play a part in a big new movie if you can talk like a robot. Try it.

Your neighbor's pet cat has just died. What do you say to your neighbor?

One-Liners

I know an artist who's so good that when he painted a mouse, his cat ate it.

Our neighbors are so stingy they charge themselves for rent.

The little strawberries were upset because their parents were in a jam.

I don't know how to drive a car, but if you want to drive a baby buggy, tickle its feet.

Our team played so badly even the other side was rooting for us.

This homework is so tough you could use it as a bullet-proof vest.

Humpty Dumpty had a terrible summer, but then he had a great fall.

It rained so hard yesterday people jumped into the lake to dry off.

My uncle is so tall he has to climb a ladder to shave himself.

Our pitcher throws balls so fast, batters have to start swinging two hours before the game starts.

A cookie jar is a "crummy" place to keep your money.

A bulldozer is what you call a bull when it's sleeping.

It was so hot yesterday even the sun went into the shade.

My dog is so mean he chased himself up a tree.

More One-Liners

George Washington was buried standing up because he never lied.

People who live in glass houses should dress in the basement.

Two twins on my block look so much alike they can't even tell themselves apart.

I sometimes snore so loudly I have to go into the other room so I won't keep myself awake.

I know two people who are such close friends, if one says "Ah," the other says "choo."

There were so many fans at the ball game last night that I almost caught a chill.

My cousins are so strong they earn a living pulling winding roads straight.

There's a place where it gets so hot the chickens lay hard-boiled eggs.

They were bragging about their horse that could count so I told them about the spelling bee.

I know someone who's so silly he thinks that a quarterback is money you get at a football game.

A sandwich thief is sometimes called a hamburglar.

A ringleader is the first one in a bathtub.

I know a town where it gets so cold even the ice shivers.

My friend's apartment building is so tall rain hits the top floor two hours before reaching the ground.

Watching a Panel Meeting

A panel is a group of people who meet to share ideas or to vote about something. To learn how to take part in a panel is to watch other people do it. You might visit a student council meeting or a meeting at City Hall, or watch a panel discussion on TV.

The chart below will help you know what to look for when studying a panel.

Name of group _____

Date of meeting _____

Place of meeting _____

Number of people on the panel _____

Purpose of meeting
( ) to vote on one or more issues
( ) to present information to the audience
( ) to answer questions from the audience

( ) Other _____

If there was a leader, what jobs did he or she do?
( ) called the meeting to order
( ) told what the meeting was about
( ) called on different people to talk
( ) decided when a vote should be taken

Who took notes at the meeting? _____

How was it decided who would have a turn to talk?
( ) whoever shouted the loudest got to talk
( ) the leader called on people

( ) Other _____
(Describe it.)

What did people in the audience do?
( ) just watched
( ) asked questions

( ) Other _____

How long did the meeting last?_____
What do you think was good about how the panel did its job?

_____

_____

Planning a Panel

To put on a play, you have to do work ahead of time. The same is true when you take part in a panel. Here are the steps to follow.

Step 1. List the people who will be on the panel:

_____

_____

_____

Step 2. Tell when your panel will meet: _____

month, day, hour

Step 3. Know how long the meeting is to last: _____

Step 4. Give the panel a name: _____

Step 5. Know the main purpose of your panel.
( ) to share what we know about the subject
( ) to figure out how to do something
( ) to answer a question by holding a vote
( ) Other _____

Step 6. Choose a chairperson who will run the meeting. The job includes starting the meeting on time and calling on people when they want to talk.

The chairperson of our panel will be: _____ .

Step 7. Choose a note taker. This person, often called the secretary, writes down what people say or do at the meeting. These notes, often called "minutes," can be shared with people who missed the meeting.

Our note taker will be: _____ .

Step 8. On another sheet of paper list what each person will have to do in order to be ready for the panel. Include a list of materials.

Step 9. Plan a real ending for your panel. The chairperson may sum up the ideas or there may be a vote.

Pantomime Starters

Putting a worm on a fishing hook
1. Take the hook from the fishing tackle box.
2. Take the worm from the bait can.
3. Start putting the worm on the hook.
4. Make a face as if it's yucky to put the worm on the hook.
5. Make up an ending.

Zipping up a jacket
1. Put on a jacket.
2. Zip it part way up.
3. See that it's stuck.
4. Try to unstick the zipper.
5. Make up an ending.

Taking a splinter out
1. Look for the splinter in your finger.
2. Take a needle and hold it in a flame to kill the germs.
3. Try digging the splinter out with the needle.
4. Use your face to show it hurts.
5. Make up an ending.

Washing a window
1. Fill a bucket with water.
2. Pour in the soap.
3. Carry the bucket to the window.
4. Wash the window.
5. Dry the window.
6. Check the window for streaks.
7. Make up an ending.

Making toast
1. Get a slice of bread.
2. Put the bread in the toaster.
3. Wait for the bread to get toasted.
4. Put butter or jam on the toast.
5. Eat it.
6. Make up an ending.

Winning a prize
1. Get the mail from the mailbox.
2. Look through the letters.
3. Get excited by one letter.
4. Tear it open.
5. Read that you've just won a million dollars.
6. Make up an ending.

Pantomime Starters

Walking the dog
1. Call the dog.
2. Put on its leash.
3. Open the door.
4. Walk along.
5. Try to keep it from chasing another dog.
6. Make up an ending.

Doing the laundry
1. Carry the dirty clothes to the washing machine.
2. Load the machine.
3. Wait around while it washes.
4. Unload the machine.
5. Make up an ending.

Pouring ketchup from a bottle
1. Open the bottle.
2. Pour.
3. Frown because nothing comes out.
4. Try many ways to get the ketchup out.
5. Make up an ending.

Fixing your hair while looking in the mirror.
1. See the mirror.
2. Study how you look.
3. Take out your comb or brush.
4. Work on your hair.
5. Make up an ending.

Waiting for a friend
1. Arrive at the place where you are to meet your friend.
2. Wait awhile.
3. Check your watch.
4. Look impatient.
5. See your friend is coming.
6. Make up an ending.

Playing a computer game
1. Find a coin in your pocket.
2. Put the coin into the machine.
3. Play the game for a while.
4. Make a face when the game is over.
5. Make up an ending.

Pantomime Starters

Reading a boring book
1. Find your place in the book.
2. Start reading.
3. Look like you're bored.
4. Try to pay attention to the book.
5. Make up an ending.

Blowing bubble gum bubbles
1. Unwrap the gum.
2. Put the gum into your mouth.
3. Chew.
4. Blow some bubbles.
5. Make up an ending.

Brushing your teeth
1. Squeeze out the last of the toothpaste from an almost-empty tube.
2. Brush your teeth.
3. Rinse your mouth out.
4. Make up an ending.

Watching a scary movie on TV
1. Check the TV listing.
2. Turn on the TV.
3. Search for the right channel.
4. Watch for a while.
5. Get scared.
6. Make up an ending.

Feeding a cat that doesn't want to eat.
1. Open the can of food.
2. Pour the food into the bowl.
3. Call the cat.
4. Try to get the cat to eat.
5. Make up an ending.

Here's the Pitch!

Here's your chance to see what it's like to be a radio sports announcer. Study the baseball pictures below. Give each team and each player a name. Then have a friend listen to you as you tell what happens in each picture. It's up to you to say whether the runner is safe or out.

Name of player #1 _____

Name of player #5 _____

Name of player #4 _____

Name of player #6 _____

Name of umpire _____

A New Sport

Here's a new game for you to describe. Study the pictures below. Make up a name for the game and each player. Then have a friend listen as you tell what happens in each picture. Your job includes making up an ending.

Name of game _____

Name of player #2 _____

Name of player #3 _____

Name of player #4 _____

Pronunciation Chalk Talks

(Write *Kansas* and *Arkansas* on the board.)

Sometimes two words look a lot alike but are said very differently. Take these two U. S. states. The first one is said "Kan zas." The second one is said "Ar kan saw." Say it with me: *Ar kan saw*.

(Write *athlete* on the board.)

People sometimes add an extra sound to a word. For example, they say *ath a leet*. The right way to say this word is *ath leet*. Say it with me: *ath leet*.

(Write *cafe* on the board.)

Some words are tricky to say because they come from foreign languages. For example, today's word—*ca fay*, which is a restaurant —comes from French. Say it with me: *ca fay*.

(Write *cement* on the board.)

Many people say the first part louder—*CE ment*—but the right way is *ce MENT*. Try it with me: *ce MENT*.

(Write *colonel* on the board.)

Today's word, which names an officer in the armed forces, used to be spoken as it looks. But over the years people came to say it this way: *kernel*, just like a kernel of corn. Say it with me: *kernel*.

(Write *Connecticut* on the board.)

Today's word is an example of trouble caused by a silent letter. The name of this U. S. state is *Con e ti kut*. Try it with me: *Con e ti kut*.

(Write *debt* on the board.)

The letter *b* is not silent in many words, but it is in *debt* —pronounced *det*—which means something that is owed. Say it with me and I'll be in your *det*. Together now: *det*.

(Write *debut* on the board.)

When something first is seen, that's called its *day byoo*. If the word seems strange, that's because it comes directly from French and in the French language, very often the final *t* is silent. Try it with me now: *day byoo*.

Pronunciation Chalk Talks

(Write *et cetera* and *etc.* on the board.)

Etc. is the abbreviation for this word (point to *et cetera*), which means "and other things." Some people mix up the *t* and *c* and say *ek se ter a*. It should be *et se ter a*. Try it: *et se ter a*.

(Write *fasten* on the board.)

Today's word means to attach. The *t* in it is silent, so the word is pronounced *fas n*.

(Write *February* on the board.)

Some people don't notice the *r* in this word. They say *Feb u ary*, but the right way to say it is *Fe bru ary*. Try it with me: *Fe bru ary*.

(Write *film* on the board.)

Some people add an extra sound to this word. They say *fil um*, but the right way to say it is *film*. Try it with me: *film*.

(Write *forbade* on the board.)

Today's word is the past tense of forbid. It's sometimes spelled *f-o-r-b-a-d* and that's a clue about how you say it: *for bad*. Try it with me: *for bad*.

(Write *genuine* on the board.)

Today's word means real. Some people put the accent on the last part of the word. They say *gen yoo INE*. The accent belongs on the first syllable: *GEN yoo in*. Say it with me: *GEN yoo in*.

(Write *government* on the board.)

Some people leave the *n* out of today's word. They say *gover ment*, but the right pronunciation is *gov ern ment*. Say it with me: *gov ern ment*.

(Write *Herb* and *herb* on the board.)

When *H-e-r-b* is spelled with a capital *H* it's the nickname for *Herbert* and you pronounce the *H*. When *h-e-r-b* is spelled with a small *h* it's a kind of plant. Then the *h* is silent. The word is *erb*. Say it: *erb*.

(Write *hiccough* and *hiccup* on the board.)

Some words are spelled two ways. For example, both groups of letters on the board spell *hiccup*. Why *h-i-c-c-o-u-g-h* is pronounced *hiccup* is a big mystery, but at least it won't fool you next time you read it.

Pronunciation Chalk Talks

(Write *Illinois* on the board.)

The last part of today's word looks something like the word *noise*. But the *s* isn't pronounced. The word, which names a U. S. state, is *Ill i noi*. Say it with me: *Ill i noi*.

(Write *island* on the board.)

The *s* in today's word is silent. Therefore, the word is pronounced *i land*. Say it with me: *i land*.

(Write *library* on the board.)

Some people skip over the first *r* in this word. They say *li berry*. The right way to pronounce it is *li brary*. Try it with me: *li brary*.

(Write *often* on the board.)

Some words have two correct pronunciations. Long ago, the only right way to say today's word was *off n*. The *t* was silent. Nowadays, while most people still say *off n*, some dictionaries say that it is also correct to say *oft n*.

(Write *pneumonia* on the board.)

In today's word, which means a disease of the lungs, the *p* is silent. The word is pronounced *noo mo ne a*. Say it with me: *noo mo ne a*.

(Write *poem* on the board.)

Some people pronounce this word as if it rhymed with *home*. But the word is spoken in two parts or syllables. It should be pronounced *po em*. Say it with me: *po em*.

(Write *sandwich* on the board.)

Some people turn the *n* and *d* of this word into an *m* sound. They say "I want a *samwich*." The right way to say the word is *sand wich*. Say it with me: *sand wich*.

(Write *somewhere* on the board.)

Today's word comes from *some* and *where*. Some people add an *s* to the end making it *somewheres*, but it should be simply *some where*. Say it with me: *some where*.

(Write *suite* on the board.)

Today's word is pronounced *sweet*. It means a group of related things. For example, an apartment is sometimes called a suite of rooms. Say the word with me: *sweet*.

(Write *umbrella* on the board.)

Some people add an *e* sound between the *b* and the *r*. They say *um ber ella*. The right way to say the word is *um brel a*. Try it with me: *um brel a*.

Question, Question, Who's Got a Question?

Learning how to ask good questions is an important skill. There are three main kinds of questions to know about.

1. A yes/no question gets a *yes* or *no* answer. An example is: "Can you count to ten?"
   Write four questions that someone might ask you that you could answer with a *yes* or *no*.

_____

_____

_____

_____

2. A *short fact* question gets a short fact for an answer—usually a number or a name. An example is: "How many brothers do you have?" You might answer with the number fact "Three."
   Write four questions that you could answer with a short fact.

_____

_____

_____

_____

3. An *open-ended* question is answered in a sentence or more. It could go on for pages and tell a long story. An example is: "How were you able to escape from the bear?" Of course, the person could answer in two words—"With luck." But the person asking the question really wants to hear the story.
   Write four questions that would take you some time to answer.

_____

_____

_____

_____

Press Conference

Speakers often must answer questions. When reporters are doing the asking, this is called a *press conference*.

You never know when you will find yourself in a press conference. It might happen if you win a prize at the Olympics or invent a new medicine or return from visiting a distant planet.

Here's your chance to practice. Imagine that you have just won a million dollars. The picture below shows a room full of reporters. Write the questions you think they'll ask in the thought balloons over their heads. Then, on the back of this sheet, write your answers to the three hardest questions.

Certificate

CERTIFICATE OF EXCELLENCE

Awarded to

_____

for excellence in public speaking in

_____

C A T E G O R Y

by

_____

How to Read an Audience

When you give a speech, you need to know how members in the audience feel about what you're saying. You can often tell by noticing what people are doing.

See for yourself. Look at the picture on *Worksheet 39* and then answer the following questions.

1. Which animals aren't paying full attention to the speaker? For each one, tell how you can tell.

_____

_____

_____

2. Which animals seem to be paying attention to the speaker? Next to each one, tell why you think so.

_____

_____

_____

_____

3. Which animal seems confused about what the speaker is saying? What makes you think so?

_____

4. Which animal seems to agree with the speaker? Explain your answer.

_____

5. Which animal seems to *dis*agree with the speaker? Tell how you know.

_____

6. Which animal seems surprised by something the speaker has said? How can you tell?

_____

7. If you were the speaker, which animal would you look at for encouragement? Explain why.

_____

How to Read an Audience

Repeat After Me

Oath to be taken by the President of the United States upon taking office

I do solemnly swear that I will faithfully execute the Office of President of the United States and will, to the best of my ability, preserve, protect and defend the Constitution of the United States.

Oath of Allegiance to the United States
(spoken as the final step in becoming a citizen)

I hereby declare, on oath, that I absolutely and entirely renounce and abjure all allegiance and fidelity to any foreign prince, potentate, state, or sovereignty, of whom or which I have heretofore been a subject or citizen; that I will support and defend the Constitution and laws of the United States against all enemies, foreign and domestic; that I will bear true faith and allegiance to the same; that I will bear arms on behalf of the United States when required by the law; or that I will perform noncombatant service in the armed forces of the United States when required by the law; or that I will perform work of national importance under civilian direction when required by the law; and that I take this obligation freely without any mental reservation or purpose of evasion; so help me God.

Oath sworn by many doctors around the world

I solemnly pledge myself to consecrate my life to the service of humanity. I will give to my teachers the respect and gratitude which is their due; I will practice my profession with conscience and dignity; the health of my patient will be my first consideration; I will respect the secrets which are confided in me; I will maintain by all means in my power the honor and the noble traditions of the medical profession; my colleagues will be my brothers; I will not permit considerations of religion, nationality, race, party politics, or social standing to intervene between my duty and my patient; I will maintain the utmost respect for human life from the time of conception; even under threat, I will not use my medical knowledge contrary to the laws of humanity. I make these promises solemnly, freely, and upon my honor.

Object Sound Cards

Animal Sound Cards

A Sound-Effects Story

Once upon a time there was a pet store. In this pet store lived a pig, a horse, a cow, a cat, a dog, a snake, a sheep, a chick, a rooster, a duck, and a lion.

One day a nice man came into the pet shop looking for a pet for his daughter. He looked closely at each animal. Then each of the animals showed the man why he or she should be picked. The pig did tricks for him, the horse gave him rides around the store, the cat sat in his lap and purred and purred, the dog chased his tail to make the man laugh, the snake did a dance to the rooster's song, the sheep gave him a sweater made from her own wool, the duck flew in a circle above his head, the chick sat on his shoulder and kept him company, and the lion juggled three eggs from the duck.

Then the whole pet shop grew very quiet as all the animals waited for the man's decision. Each wished that he would be chosen to be a pet for the man's daughter. The man looked at every animal and then went up to the pet store owner and paid him a great deal of money. Then the man turned to the animals and told them that all of them would be pets for his daughter. Everyone rejoiced and lived happily to the end of their days.

Anna Suid

Talking and Listening on the Job

Many people have to be good at talking. Others need to be good at listening. Some have to do both. See for yourself. After the jobs on this page, write a sentence that tells why the person has to be good at speaking or listening or both. If you like, use another sheet of paper to give your answers.

banker _____

cab driver _____

dentist/ _____
   doctor

jury member _____

lawyers _____

magician _____

minister/ _____
   priest/rabbi

parent _____

pilot _____

plumber _____

police officer _____

reporter _____

salesperson _____

sports coach _____

teacher _____

waiter/ _____
   waitress

The Speech Game

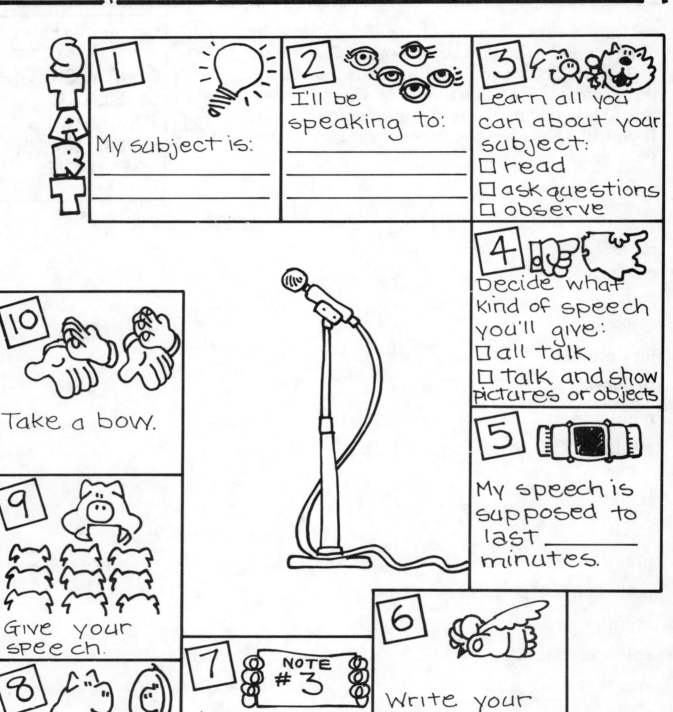

START

1 My subject is:
_____
_____

2 I'll be speaking to:
_____
_____

3 Learn all you can about your subject:
☐ read
☐ ask questions
☐ observe

4 Decide what kind of speech you'll give:
☐ all talk
☐ talk and show pictures or objects

5 My speech is supposed to last _____ minutes.

6 Write your speech.

7 How will you give your speech?
☐ read it
☐ talk from notes

NOTE #3

8 Rehearse your speech.

9 Give your speech.

10 Take a bow.

Breaking a Subject into Pieces

The *subject* is what your speech is all about. When you give a speech, you can't tell about your subject all at once. Instead, you do it piece by piece. The main pieces of a subject are called topics. To keep the topics in order, it sometimes helps to make an outline.

1. Complete the following outline about bicycles. The Roman numerals are for the main topics. The letters (A, B, C, and so on) are for the smaller topics, sometimes called subtopics. List at least three subtopics under each main topic.

Bicycles

I. Parts of a bicycle

    A.

    B.

    C.

    D.

    E.

II. Uses of a bicycle

    A.

    B.

    C.

    D.

    E.

2. Make an outline of any subject you know something about. It can be a sport, a school subject, or anything. Break the subject into two or three main topics. Under each of these main topics, list at least two subtopics. Be sure to give the outline a title. When it's finished, it should look something like the outline on bicycles.

How to Rehearse a Speech

If you want to give a good speech, you have to *rehearse*. This means practicing it over and over the way a musician practices a song. This way, when you give the speech for real, the audience will enjoy it more... and so will you.

Check each box ☐ when you've done the step.

Step 1. Rehearse the speech by yourself.

Listen to yourself give the speech aloud at least twice. If you have any trouble saying a word, look it up in the dictionary or ask someone to help you. Practice holding up any pictures or objects you plan to show.

☐ First by-yourself rehearsal

☐ Second by-yourself rehearsal

List any words to watch out for: _____

_____

Step 2. Now give the speech again and check to see that it lasts the right amount of time.

☐ The speech took just the right amount of time.

☐ The speech was too short so I added _____

☐ The speech was too long so I left out _____

Step 3. Rehearse the speech in front of a trial audience. Ask for ways to improve your speech.

Write the most important suggestion given you: _____

_____

Speech Review Checklist

Name of speaker _____ Name of speech _____

Date _____ Audience _____

Overall

What was best about the speech? _____

_____

What needed the most improvement? _____

_____

Details

Did the *beginning* grab attention? _____

Which *ideas* were the most interesting? _____

_____

What should have been added or left out? _____

Were the ideas in an *order* that was easy to follow? _____

Should any ideas have been moved? Explain. _____

Did the speech have a real *ending*? _____

Was the *voice* too loud, too soft, or just right? _____

Were there enough *props* (pictures, objects)? _____

Was the *talking speed* too fast, too slow, or just right? _____

Was there enough *eye contact*? _____

How was the speaker's *posture*? _____

Were the *hand gestures* helpful or confusing? _____

How to Present a Children's Book

Step 1. Know the age of the audience.

I'll be reading for children who are _____ years old.

Step 2. Read at least two books that would interest your audience. Ask a librarian to help you pick the books. Write the book you like best here and tell why you chose it.

I'll read _____ by _____
                        (name of book)   (author)

because _____
                         (Tell what you like about the book.)

Step 3. Plan what you'll say to the audience to get them interested in hearing you read the book.

I'll say _____

_____

Step 4. Practice reading the book at least three times to yourself. This practice should include holding up the book to show the pictures. (Hint: Many storytellers read the page *before* showing the picture.)
Practice #1 ☐   Practice #2 ☐   Practice #3 ☐

Step 5. Read the book to a friend and ask how you can do better.

Suggestion: _____

Step 6. Read the book to a real audience. On the back of this paper write a few words that tell what was good about your reading. Then tell how you could do better next time.

Telephone Calling Scripts

Before you make a telephone call, it's a good idea to plan what you want to say. This makes it easier for you and the other person.

1. Fill in the blanks and write an ending for the telephone scripts below.
    A. Shopping

    Hello, I'm wondering if your store has _____.
    (Name the product.)

    (pause) Do you have it in _____ ?
    (Give the size or color you want.)

    I need to know how much it costs. _____

    _____
    (Write an ending.)

    B. Planning to meet with someone for studying, seeing a movie, etc.
    Hello, _____, this is _____ .
    (name of person)(your name)

    I wonder if you would like to _____.
    (Say what you want to do.)

    When? Well, I was thinking of _____
    (Give day and time.)

    _____ .
    (Write an ending.)

    C. Calling for help in an emergency such as a fire or illness

    Hello, is this the _____?
    (name of group whose help you want)

    There's _____
    (You complete it.)

2. On the back of this sheet write scripts for the following calls:
    A. to make a doctor or dentist appointment
    B. to find a fact by calling the library
    C. to invite guests to a party
    D. to turn down an invitation you received to a party

Tongue Twisters

A noisy noise annoys an oyster.

Big backed bumblebees buzz.

Crickets cry.

Four fat frogs fried fritters for food.

Flatten flattering fleas.

Six slippery seals sell sleds.

Silent slugs slither.

Selfish shellfish shilly-shally.

Gray geese greet gazing Greeks.

Sixty-six sickly sailors.

Bedbugs bleed blue blood.

Wild wolves roam wintry windy wastes.

Unique New Yorkers yodel.

Soldiers' shoulders shudder.

Praise braids.

Nibble noodles.

Brown bread burns badly.

This is a zither.

Remember really rural roads?

Some shun sunshine.

She says she shall sew sheets.

Rush the washing, Russell.

Which is the witch that wished the wicked wish?

Round and round the rugged rock the ragged rascal ran.

Boys, bring books back.

Cross crossings cautiously.

Look Who's Talking

Like a musical instrument, your voice can make many different sounds. See—or *hear*—for yourself.

1. Write the exact same words over the heads of the following characters. For example, each of them could be saying "I'm hungry." Now, make up a different voice for each of the characters. One might talk slow and loud; another fast and soft. When the voices sound right to your ear, try them out on someone else. See if that person can match the voices with the pictures.

2. Try drawing other characters on the back of this sheet. Make up voices for these characters.

Report on the Weather Reporter

A good way to learn how to give a report is to watch other people do it, but you need to look *carefully*. The chart below will help you study what a TV weather reporter does. For each question, make a check mark or write in a few words. To check the time, you'll need a watch with a second hand.

Chart

1. Beginning: How does the weather person start the report?
   ☐ A. with a summary of the weather ☐ C. in some other way: _____

   ☐ B. with a joke _____

2. Materials: What visual materials (props) does the reporter use?
   ☐ A. maps ☐ C. other things: _____

   ☐ B. photographs _____

3. Tone of voice: What kind of voice did the reporter use?
   ☐ A. serious ☐ C. other: _____

   ☐ B. silly _____

4. Pacing: How fast did the reporter talk?
   ☐ A. fast throughout ☐ C. slow throughout
   ☐ B. medium throughout ☐ D. mixed

5. Eyes: Where does the weather person look?
   ☐ A. at the viewers ☐ C. at both the props and
   ☐ B. at the props   the viewers

6. Gestures: What hand gestures does the weather person make?
   ☐ A. points ☐ C. other gestures: _____

   ☐ B. waves _____

7. Ending: How does the reporter end the report?
   ☐ A. with a summary ☐ C. in some other way: ____

   ☐ B. with a joke _____

8. Time: How long did the report last (in minutes and seconds)? _____

Weather Puppets

SUNNY   CLOUDY   LIGHTNING

WINDY   SNOW   FLOOD

FOG   RAIN   HEAT

Ear It Is

BULLETIN BOARDS

CAGING STAGE FRIGHT

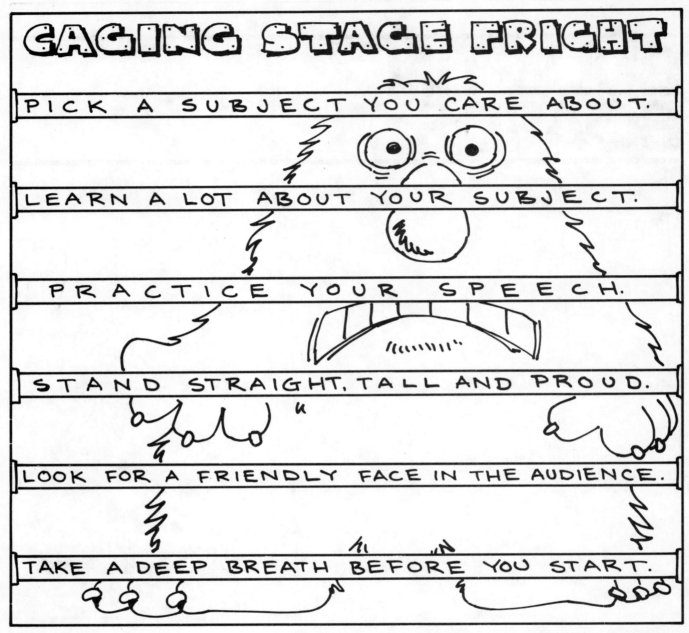

PICK A SUBJECT YOU CARE ABOUT.

LEARN A LOT ABOUT YOUR SUBJECT.

PRACTICE YOUR SPEECH.

STAND STRAIGHT, TALL AND PROUD.

LOOK FOR A FRIENDLY FACE IN THE AUDIENCE.

TAKE A DEEP BREATH BEFORE YOU START.

Studies have shown that public-speaking raises anxiety in most people. One way to help students get stage-fright under control is to face it openly. You might even have students give one-minute talks about what they feel when standing before the class. It's comforting to know that other people share some of our anxieties.

The Faces of a STORYTELLER

When you tell a story, your face can show what the characters look like. Use the mirror to practice the faces listed here.

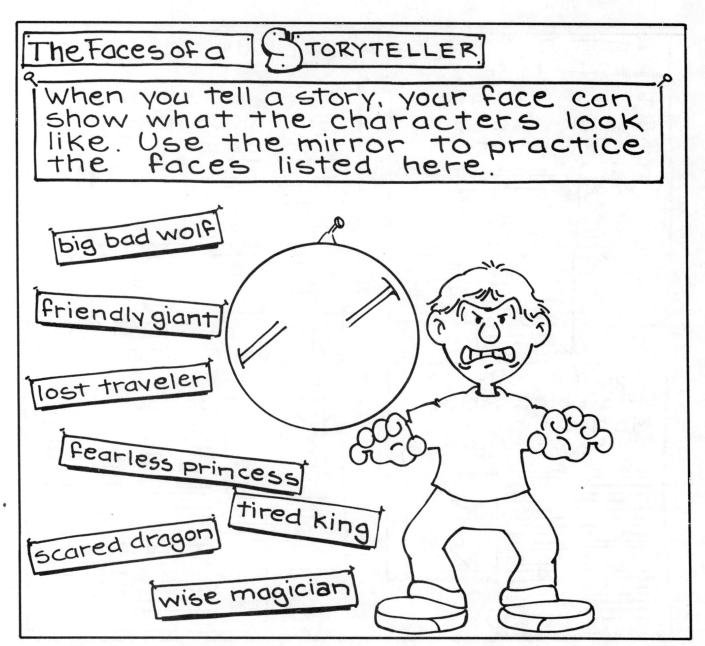

big bad wolf

friendly giant

lost traveler

fearless princess

tired king

scared dragon

wise magician

Feedback is essential for all stage presentations. The advantage of using the mirror is that it promotes *self-*evaluation.

For more on storytelling, see the Storytelling activity.

To help students learn that speaking skills make a difference in the real world, collect or, better, have students collect, a month's worth of newspaper articles about local, national, and international speeches. As a follow-up, your students might write to these newsmaking speakers asking for copies of their speeches that could be read aloud and studied in your class.

PRONUNCIATION PUZZLERS

Many English words are not spoken the way they are spelled. How do you think the words on this board are said? You'll find the answers under the flaps.

GNU
an animal

HERB
a plant

QUICHE
a cheese pie

CUPBOARD
a place to store food

LIEUTENANT
an officer in the army

The answers under the flap are:
   gnu = nu (the g is silent)
   herb = erb (the h is silent)
   quiche = keesh
   cupboard = cubboard
   lieutenant = lew-tenant
This bulletin board is meant to interest students in correct pronunciation. You can expand the list of words simply by noting pronunciation problems in the room.

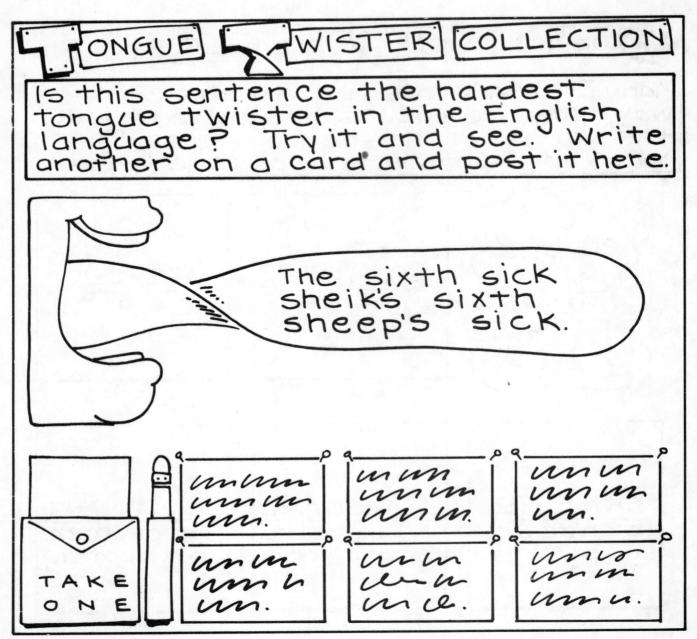

TONGUE TWISTER COLLECTION

Is this sentence the hardest tongue twister in the English language? Try it and see. Write another on a card and post it here.

The sixth sick sheik's sixth sheep's sick.

TAKE ONE

This is a group-made bulletin board. For more suggestions on developing articulation skills, see Tongue (Un)Twisting in the lessons section of this book.

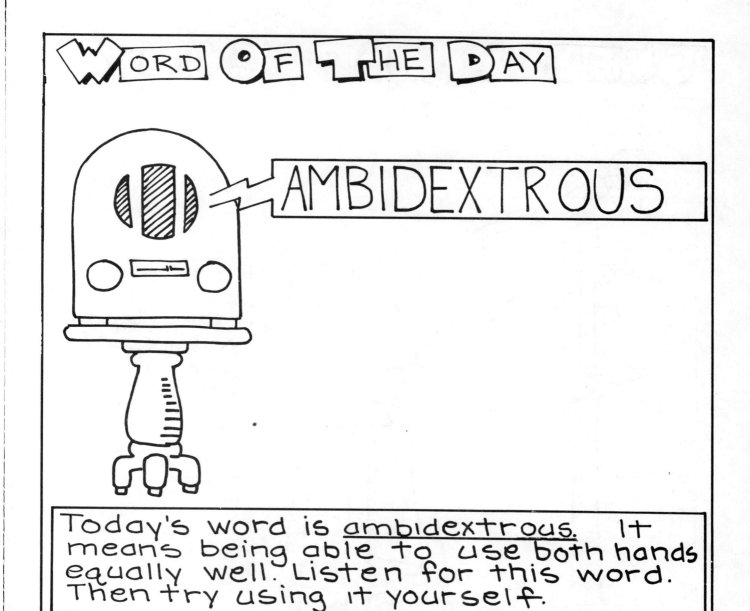

WORD OF THE DAY

AMBIDEXTROUS

Today's word is <u>ambidextrous.</u> It means being able to use both hands equally well. Listen for this word. Then try using it yourself.

Every day post a relatively unusual word along with its definition. Then, the students are to listen for the word which you will manage to use several times. Whenever students hear it, they are to raise their hands or otherwise signal you.

If it's too much of a chore to present a new word daily, either assign the work to the students (who then would be responsible for about a word a month), or do the activity weekly.

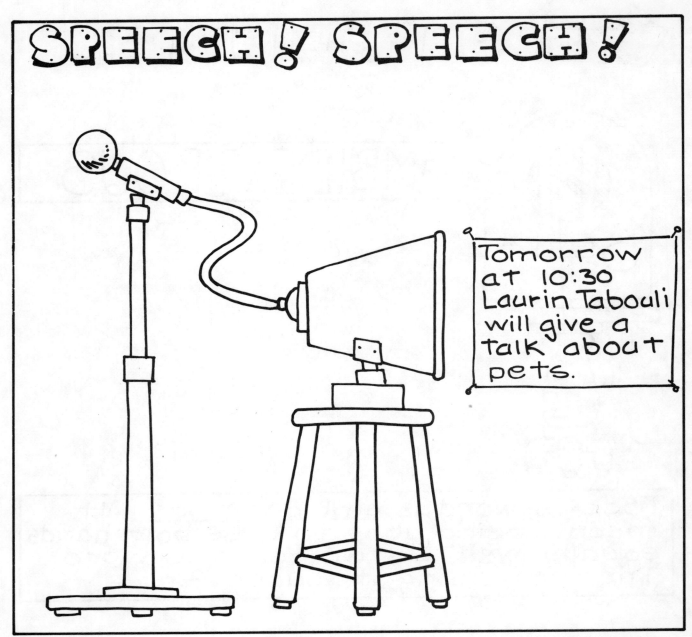

Serious speeches deserve a little publicity. Treat a major classroom speech—whether an oral report or a poetry reading—as a real event. Draw attention to it via a permanent speech announcement bulletin board.

In addition, you might have students hand out broadsides or mount posters concerning speeches of school-wide interest. Such speeches would be delivered in the auditorium or done as a lecture series presented in many classrooms.

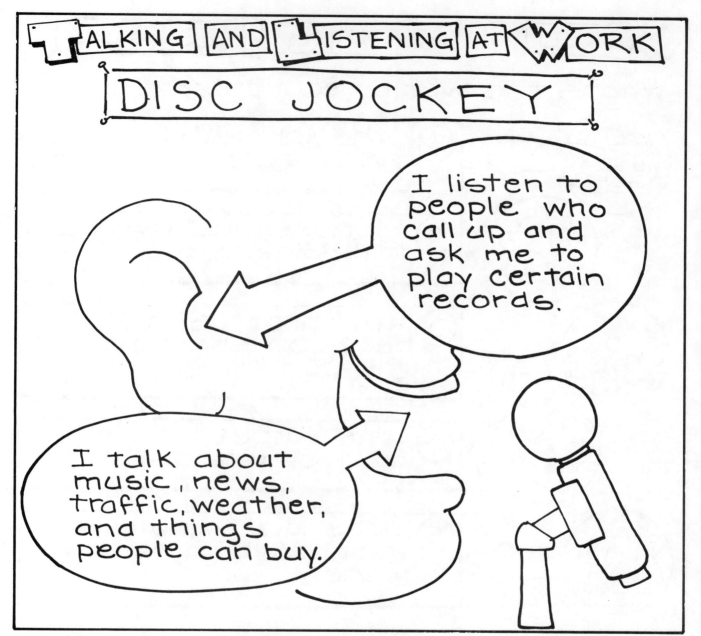

This bulletin board focuses on the vocational aspects of speaking and listening. Keep the lips and ear in place but change the message weekly or monthly. The teacher can write the words, but how much better it will be if the students do the work. For a related project, see Speaking of Speaking and Listening in the lessons section of this book.

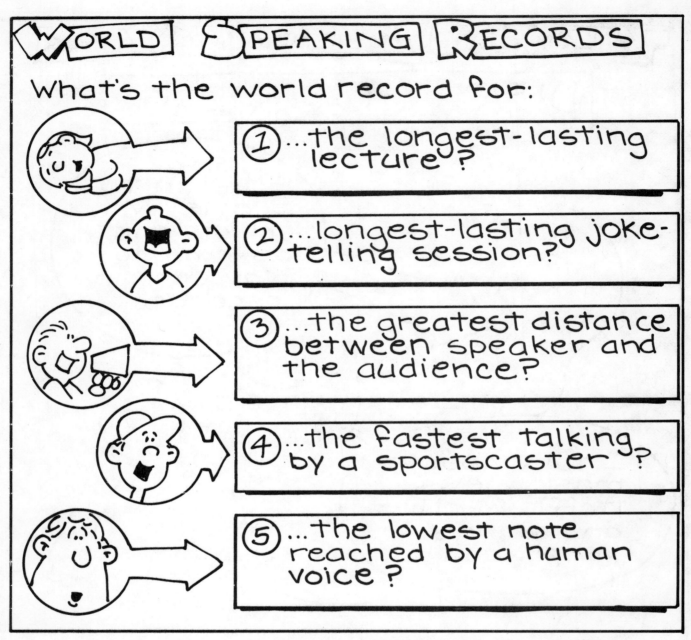

WORLD SPEAKING RECORDS

What's the world record for:

① ...the longest-lasting lecture?

② ...longest-lasting joke-telling session?

③ ...the greatest distance between speaker and the audience?

④ ...the fastest talking by a sportscaster?

⑤ ...the lowest note reached by a human voice?

Answers, to be printed under the flaps, are:
1. 56 hours
2. 16 hours
3. From the moon to the earth, a distance of over 200,000 miles
4. Gerry Wilmot, describing hockey, spoke 176 words in 30 seconds.
5. Singer Roy Hart has sung notes lower than the lowest note on a piano.

A possible follow-up would be to stage your own "speech-record" competition. Categories could include: Longest poem memorized, quickest clearly articulated rendering of a local radio ad, most accurate imitation of a natural or manufactured sound. For a useful resource, see *The Guinness Book of World Records*.